Draw NASCAR

DATE DUE		
OCT 0 2 2008	MAY 2 7 2010	
OCT 1 6 2008	MAY 1 6 2012	
NOV 1 3 2008		
SEP 2 8 2009		
OCT 1 5 2009		
NOV 2010		
MAY 2 4 2012		
FEB 1 6 2011		

DRAW ///////NASCAR®

T 1629370

► ► ► **LEE HAMMOND**

NORTH LIGHT BOOKS
CINCINNATI, OHIO

www.artistsnetwork.com

About the Author

Lee Hammond has been a professional artist and art instructor for more than twenty years and a published author for ten years. She owned and operated the Midwest School of Art in Lenexa, Kansas, for five years. She since has built a private studio in Overland Park, Kansas, where she continues to teach part time. She also conducts drawing seminars, gives school lectures and mentors nationwide. Lee also is a certified Police Composite Artist, currently on call for the Kansas City metro area. She has worked for the television show *America's Most Wanted*. Lee has three children, Shelly, LeAnne and Christopher and three grandchildren, Taylor, Caitlynn and Gavyn.

Lee has written thirteen North Light books on drawing techniques and has been a contributing writer for *The Artist's Magazine*. She is licensed with many of NASCAR's racing teams. Fine art prints of her portraits of drivers are sold on www.nascar.com and www.leehammond.com and in various magazines, such as *Racing Milestones* and *Winston Cup Weekly*.

Lee Hammond, Inc.
PO Box 24007
Shawnee Mission, KS 66283
(913) 402-1ART
RaceArtByLee@aol.com
www.leehammond.com

Other fine North Light books are available from your local bookstore, art supply store or direct from the publisher.

08 07 06 05 04   5 4 3 2 1

Library of Congress Cataloging in Publication Data
Hammond, Lee.
    Draw NASCAR / Lee Hammond—1st ed.
        p. cm.
    Includes index.
    ISBN 1-58180-483-0 (pbk. : alk. paper)
    1. Automobiles, Racing, in art. 2. Colored pencil drawing—Technique. I. Title.

Nc825.A8 H36 2004   2003054083
743'.997967—dc21   CIP

Edited by Amanda Metcalf and Vanessa Lyman
Cover design by Nicole Armstrong
Interior design by Wendy Dunning
Interior layout by John Langan
Production coordinated by Mark Griffin

METRIC CONVERSION CHART

To convert	to	multiply by
Inches	Centimeters	2.54
Centimeters	Inches	0.4
Feet	Centimeters	30.5
Centimeters	Feet	0.03
Yards	Meters	0.9
Meters	Yards	1.1
Sq. Inches	Sq. Centimeters	6.45
Sq. Centimeters	Sq. Inches	0.16
Sq. Feet	Sq. Meters	0.09
Sq. Meters	Sq. Feet	10.8
Sq. Yards	Sq. Meters	0.8
Sq. Meters	Sq. Yards	1.2
Pounds	Kilograms	0.45
Kilograms	Pounds	2.2
Ounces	Grams	28.3
Grams	Ounces	0.035

Dedication

This book is dedicated to Tony Stewart, the 2002 NASCAR Winston Cup Champion. Congratulations, Tony, on a wonderful career and a title well deserved.

I want to personally thank Tony Stewart, and all of the wonderful people at Joe Gibbs Racing for helping me launch my career in NASCAR. Without their belief in my abilities, and the kindness they have extended me, I would not be where I am today. A heartfelt thank-you to Cheryl, Mandy, Sue, Mickey, Paige, Bobby and Joe for always making me feel like family. It is truly an honor to work with you all.

Thank you, Tony, for allowing me to illustrate your awesome career and for making me feel like part of the team!

Tony Stewart, 2002 NASCAR Winston Cup Champion

It's no easy accomplishment to win a NASCAR Winston Cup championship. The title is determined by the number of points accumulated during the season. Points are distributed for various reasons. Any driver who leads in a race earns 5 points. The driver who leads the most laps gets 5 more bonus points. Every driver who finishes the race accumulates points based on his position, the top spot earning 175 points. In the event of a tie at the end of the season, the driver with the most wins gains the title.

Tony Stewart earned 4,800 points in 2002 to become NASCAR Winston Cup champion. Mark Martin earned 4,762 for second place—that's only a 38 point difference! A driver who has an injury or car problems or doesn't do well may not even qualify for many races and will acquire very few points. Geoffrey Bodine, for example, was injured in a NASCAR Craftsman Truck race during the season and missed a lot of racing. He finished 2002 with only 803 points. Quite a spread!

Acknowledgments

"No success is ever achieved alone." No statement could be truer of my success, especially in my career with NASCAR. Like the entire NASCAR industry, this has been a team effort from the very beginning.

I also need to acknowledge my friends who have spent countless hours to help make Lee Hammond Inc. a fine running machine. Without Jeff Osborne, Laura Tiedt, Jay Vannice, Paul Linder, Kyle Elliott, Joy Osborne, Ashley Udden, Todd Cletcher, Jim Fvetlecic and Craig Hill, nothing would ever get done.

A huge thank-you also is in order to everyone involved with NASCAR who has placed faith in me to represent the sport and drivers. They have guided me through a very complicated industry and mentored me so I feel like I belong. Not since I began working with North Light Books have I encountered a better group of people to associate with. It is thrilling to take an established career like the one I have developed with North Light Books and blend it with such an exciting field.

I want to thank everyone at North Light for coming along for the ride and for allowing me to take you with me into my new career pursuits. We have had a long, successful career together, and I look forward to many more creative years.

Thank you, Amanda Metcalf, Pam Wissman, Vanessa Lyman, and Julia Groh, for working with me so closely to create such an awesome book. Thank you David Lewis for continuing to believe in me and giving me these opportunities!

Racing Enthusiasts

I want to thank Sam Mohamed as the first person to encourage me to enter this sport. His knowledge of the sport and encouragement made it fun and interesting. This is a drawing of Sam and me at my first NASCAR Winston Cup race in Texas in 1999. You can see the racetrack and the crowd reflected in my sunglasses. This is where it all began.

Foreword

If you had told me five years ago that I would be licensed with NASCAR and would be one of the leading illustrators specializing in racing illustration, I would have laughed hysterically! Nothing could have been further from my mind. In fact, I was not a fan of the sport at all! I never watched the races, let alone knew who the drivers were. (Forgive me, guys!)

My only real exposure to the sport occurred when I was a young girl growing up in Lincoln, Nebraska. My older brother, Bill Hagen, drove stock cars there at the local track. I remember watching the excitement through the fence as he roared around with his blue car kicking up dust. The closest thing I got to race art was a feeble attempt to make a homemade trophy for Bill with a metal car and a piece of wood.

Five years ago, my career was set. I owned a successful art school and art supply store and had an established career with North Light Books. I taught more than three hundred students a week out of my very own textbooks! Everything was running smoothly. That is, until my friend Sam Mohamed introduced me to NASCAR.

Sam was and is a NASCAR junkie. He lives and breathes it. I thought he was nuts. But as an auto mechanic, he was as passionate about racing as I was about art. Not being able to imagine my life without my artwork, that type of dedication was something I could clearly understand. I decided to give racing a try, so I watched the races with him one Sunday.

Sam narrated the races as we watched, sharing his vast knowledge of the sport. He explained the technical

Rusty Wallace

It was Sam's devotion to NASCAR and Rusty Wallace that led me to draw my first racing illustration of Rusty in 1999 as a birthday present for Sam. Who knew that it would launch me into such a fast-paced career!

aspects, the history, the point system, the various tracks and their differences. But most of all he introduced me to the personalities of NASCAR. In time I began to take a strong interest in the drivers—and the sport—and dedicated every Sunday to watching the races.

I decided to do something special for Sam, and I made my very first drawing with a NASCAR theme. I found some photos of Sam's favorite driver, Rusty Wallace, and his car and compiled them into a drawing. I really

enjoyed creating it, and Sam loved it. I started to draw a different driver every weekend as we watched races together. My collection grew along with my interest in the sport. Sam saw a career move in my future.

It wasn't long before the entrepreneur in me rose up. I had to find out if I had a chance in the field of NASCAR illustration. I boarded a plane to Charlotte, North Carolina, and, as the old saying goes … the rest is history!

Table of Contents

NASCAR.

Ward Burton

Ward Burton began racing karts when he was eight years old. In 1990 he joined the NASCAR Busch Series. In 1994 he competed for rookie of the year in the NASCAR Winston Cup, driving alongside his brother, Jeff Burton. Ward has earned five career NASCAR Winston Cup victories, and won at least one race in 2000, 2001 and 2002. He is an avid environmentalist and founded the Ward Burton Wildlife Foundation to conserve and protect wildlife habitats.

You Can Do It!

This is more than just a how-to-draw book. It's also an informational book filled with facts about America's fastest growing sport: NASCAR! I'll take you from the sandy shores of Daytona to the superspeedways of today, explaining the details that make this sport so fun and interesting. By the end, you'll not only be able to draw the action, you'll understand what makes NASCAR work.

Each illustration will teach you two things. First, I'll show you how the art was created, explaining the methods, colors and techniques. You'll understand what tools I used and what approach I took to make it look the way it does. Second, I'll describe what the illustration depicts, offering facts about the car, the driver or that particular race. You'll learn history, technical details and driver facts.

Learn the art, learn the sport. It's all in here!

YOU CAN IMPROVE

I've had the pleasure of teaching art for more than twenty years. I've seen all of the struggles and frustrations artists go through as they develop. It takes time, as does anything, to become proficient in drawing. I've developed a proven system of teaching that will give you the success you're looking for.

When I was a beginning artist using colored pencil for the first time, my drawings looked like those on a kindergarten classroom wall. The results were less than impressive, resembling nothing more than crayon renderings. Anyone who draws at all has suffered through that awkward stage, but with time I was able to control the pencils to create

the look I wanted. So can you! I can help you get to that level.

Drawing shapes accurately is essential for drawing realistically, and the methods provided in this book will take the mystery out it. All you need is patience and practice. Take the book as it comes, page by page. Your shapes will improve immediately. I'll also provide color recipes through color names and color combinations. I'll show you different ways of applying colored pencil to achieve different looks and textures. Again, practice will be the key to your success.

Let me guide you through the learning process. You'll be drawing the essence and illusion of NASCAR before you know it! And, everything you learn here will carry over to other drawing subject matters as well.

Before
My fourteen-year-old son, Christopher, drew this freehand drawing of Ward Burton's #22 Cat Dodge.

After
After some guidance from me about using graphing methods to create more accurate shapes, he made this drawing which looks much more realistic. Learning how to use the pencils properly gives the drawing a more polished appearance.
    You can have the same success.

Chapter One

GETTING STARTED

Choosing Pencils

It's important to know how the various brands of colored pencils differ. The term colored pencil is somewhat deceptive, implying they are all alike. However, not all of them feel, look or are applied the same way. Each brand of pencils produces different effects and requires different techniques for application. You must decide which brand will create the look you want your artwork to have.

When drawing the essence of NASCAR, I generally use two brands: Verithin and Prismacolor. Both are manufactured by the same company, but they differ in their application.

PRISMACOLOR PENCILS

Prismacolors have a thick, soft, wax-based lead that provides a heavy application of color. They are opaque and will completely cover the paper surface. They are excellent for achieving smooth, shiny surfaces and brilliant colors. The colors blend easily to produce an almost "painted" appearance to your work.

VERITHIN PENCILS

Verithins have hard, thin lead that is dry with a low wax content. They give a grainy appearance, allowing the texture of the paper to come through. They also maintain a sharp point, so they're good for detail lines and edges. I use them when applying backgrounds and drawing small decals and lettering. Verithins are good for layering colors when you don't want the colors to actually mix together.

Instead of the "painted" feel of Prismacolor pencils, Verithin pencils yield more of a "drawn" look. They're compatible with Prismacolor but are more limited in range of colors at thirty-six.

NERO PENCILS

Using the Nero clay-based black pencil is an excellent way to achieve deep, rich black in your work without a hazy wax buildup. This is the blackest pigment I've ever found in a colored pencil. It comes in five degrees of hardness, ranging from soft (1) to hard (5).

Prismacolor Pencils

Verithin Pencils

Nero Pencil

The Look of Verithin Pencils

I did all of these drawings with Verithin pencils. Some people like the sketchy look these pencils provide, saying it looks more artistic.

Driver Tim Flock Leads the Race in the Sand in Florida
The grainy appearance of Verithin pencils works well to create "vintage" looking drawings, so I used one for this drawing of vintage NASCAR cars.

8" × 10" (20cm × 25cm)
Verithin pencil on no. 3297 arctic white mat board

COLOR USED

Verithin. Dark Umber.

Curtis Turner Driving a 1957 Ford Fairlane
Again, the vintage feel worked for this subject, especially because it's black and white.

8" × 10" (20cm × 25cm)
Verithin pencil on no. 3297 arctic white mat board

COLOR USED

Verithin. Black.

NASCAR'S STORY

Dale Earnhardt drove this car to victory on July 19, 1974 at Metrolina Speedway in North Carolina. It was his very first win on an asphalt track and it paved the way to an impressive career that earned him seven NASCAR Winston Cup Championships.

Dale Earnhardt Driving a 1964 Chevelle

Study this drawing carefully to see the hallmark signs of Verithin pencils. Can you see their grainy effect? The dry, non-waxy application lets you layer one color over another without the pencil color building up. Using firmer pressure gives you deeper tones, as on the tires and the 8. Pressure causes the pigment to "fill in" and create a solid tone that isn't grainy. However, these pencils are not good for filling in large areas with deep, solid tone. To create rich, brilliant color, I always switch to Prismacolor.

8" × 10" (20cm × 25cm)
Verithin, Prismacolor and Nero pencils on no. 3297 Arctic White mat board

NASCAR'S STORY

You may wonder how these cars fit in with NASCAR. They're called Modifieds and are the only cars in NASCAR that have open wheels instead of fenders. They resemble the sprint cars that many of the NASCAR drivers drove when they were young and just beginning their careers.

NASCAR's Featherlite Modified Series

This drawing has a sketchier appearance but is a fun example of what you can do with Verithin pencils.

9" × 12" (23cm × 30cm)
Verithin pencils on no. 1009 Light Jonquil mat board

The Look of Prismacolor Pencils

The drawings on this page were done with Prismacolor pencils. Notice the sleek, solid look of the colors.

When using Prismacolor pencils, especially dark colors, a foggy haze may appear on your work as the wax of the pencil rises to the surface. You can gently rub it with your finger as you draw to keep it from showing. To make it go away permanently, spray your work with workable fixative when you're through.

Richard Petty's STP Chevrolet
To create the brilliant colors of Richard's car and the shiny look, I always use Prismacolor pencils. Look at how smooth and even the color looks. The pigment applies heavily, completely filling the paper surface. Note that this drawing is done on a colored surface, but the Prismacolor lead is thick and opaque enough that even white can cover the gray board completely.

8" × 10" (20cm × 25cm)
Prismacolor pencil on no. 1052 Blue Gray mat board

COLORS USED

Prismacolor. Aquamarine, Black, Cool Gray 70%, Mediterranean Blue, Poppy Red, True Blue, White.

Richard Petty
One of the most remembered paint schemes of the late seventies was the very recognizable red and blue colors of Richard Petty. With two hundred career victories and seven NASCAR Winston Cup championships, Richard will always be known as "The King." For many, his name is synonymous with NASCAR.

Richard Petty—The King
20" × 16"
(51cm × 41cm)
Prismacolor pencils on Suede mat board

Jeff Gordon's Dupont Chevrolet

This drawing of Jeff Gordon's Dupont Chevro-let shows how brilliant the vehicles of NASCAR have become.

To create visual impact with this drawing, I cropped it to show only a portion of the car. The result is an interesting drawing that focuses on the number 24. I love the color in the background, especially around the front tire. It creates the illusion of shadow and light around the car.

6½" × 7" (17cm × 18cm)
Prismacolor pencil on no. 971 Daffodil mat board

COLORS USED

Prismacolor. Aquamarine, Black, Canary Yellow, Copenhagen Blue, Crimson Red, Mediterranean Blue, Poppy Red, True Blue, White, Indigo Blue, Magenta, Periwinkle.

Jeff Gordon

Decals are an important aspect of NASCAR. It's almost impossible to draw them freehand with complete accuracy because they are so small.

The most recognizable part of a team and driver's image is the driver's number. You can see how I used the 24 to create a composition in this portrait of Jeff Gordon.

16" × 20" (41cm × 51cm)
Prismacolor pencil on suede mat board

NASCAR'S STORY

Jeff Gordon debuted in the NASCAR Winston Cup Series in 1992. Within eight years he had acquired four NASCAR Winston Cup Championships. His team was once called "The Rainbow Warriors" due to the bright recognizable paint schemes they use on their cars.

The Combination Look

Achieving different looks in one drawing requires a combination of pencils. For example, I like the bright, solid look of Prismacolor pencils, but I rarely use them to draw faces due to their heavy nature. I use Verithin pencils when drawing a driver's portrait and Prismacolor pencils for the vehicle and uniform. For more information on drawing faces, see my book *Drawing in Color: People and Portraits*.

NASCAR'S STORY

Ken Schrader, a St. Louis native, was one of the first drivers to follow open-wheel racing with a career in stock car racing. He began his career driving short tracks with Sprints and Midget racing in the Midwest. In 1985, he won the NASCAR Winston Cup Rookie of the Year title. He continues to compete in the NASCAR Winston Cup Series in addition to many other forms of racing.

Ken Schrader

In this piece, you can clearly see where I used both the Prismacolor and the Verithin pencils. I needed bright colors to create the brilliant colors of the car and Ken Schrader's uniform, so I used Prismacolor pencils. The grainy feel of Verithin pencils suited the face and the edge of the background. I filled in the background with Black Prismacolor pencil, proving how heavy and opaque these pencils really are.

Ken Schrader
20" x 16" (51cm x 41cm)
Verithin and Prismacolor pencils on no. 1008 Ivory mat board

Choosing a Drawing Surface

As with anything we do, the quality of our work is determined by the quality of the tools we employ for the job.

The paper you use with colored pencils is critical to your success. There are many fine papers on the market today. You have hundreds of options of sizes, colors and textures. As you try various types, you will undoubtedly develop your personal favorites.

Before I will even try a paper for colored pencil, I always check the weight. Although there are many beautiful papers available, I feel many of them are just too thin to work with. I learned this the hard way, after I did a beautiful drawing of my daughter only to have the paper buckle when I picked it up. The crease formed was permanent, and no amount of framing kept my eye from focusing on it first. From

that point on, I never used a paper that could easily bend when picked up. The more rigid, the better! Strathmore has many papers that I often use. I've included the papers and mat boards I personally like to use the most and recommend to my students.

PAPERS

Artagain is a recycled paper by Strathmore that has somewhat of a flannel appearance to it. This 60-lb. (130gsm) cover-weight paper comes in a good variety of colors. Although it has a speckled appearance, its surface has no noticeable texture. It is available in both pads and single sheets for larger projects.

Renewal is another Strathmore paper, very similar to Artagain, but it has the look of fibers in it instead of speckles. I like it for its soft earth tones.

MAT BOARDS

My personal favorite is Crescent because of the firmness of the board. It is already rigid and doesn't have to be taped down to a drawing board. This makes it very easy to transport in a portfolio. Its wide range of colors and textures is extremely attractive. Not only do I match the color to the subject I am drawing, I will often use the same color of mat board when framing the piece to make it color coordinated.

Crescent Suede Board is another one of my favorites. It has a surface like suede or velveteen.

Regular mat boards are mildly acidic, which will cause the quality of the art to degrade over a period of time. If you prefer, acid-free archival quality paper is available for a little extra money.

Papers

Mat Boards

Other Tools of the Trade

PENCIL SHARPENERS

Pencil sharpeners are very important with colored pencils. Later in the book, you will see how many of the techniques require a very sharp point at all times. I prefer an electric sharpener, or a battery-operated one when traveling. A hand-held sharpener requires a twisting motion of the arm. This is usually what breaks off the pencil points. The motor-driven sharpeners allow you to insert the pencil straight on, reducing breakage. If you still prefer a hand-held sharpener, spend the extra money for a good metal one with replacement blades.

ERASERS

I suggest that you have three different erasers to use with colored pencils: a kneaded eraser, a Pink Pearl eraser and a typewriter eraser. Although colored pencil is very difficult, if not impossible, to erase, the erasers can be used to soften colors as you draw.

The kneaded eraser is like a squishy piece of rubber, good for removing your initial line drawing as you work. Because of its soft, pliable quality, it will not damage or rough up your paper surface.

The Pink Pearl eraser is a good eraser for general cleaning. I use it the most when I am cleaning large areas, such as backgrounds. It is also fairly easy on the paper surface.

The typewriter eraser looks like a pencil with a little brush on the end of it. It is a highly abrasive eraser, good for removing stubborn marks from the paper. It can also be used to get into tight places or to create clean edges. However, great care must be taken when using this eraser, because it can easily damage the paper and leave a hole.

MECHANICAL PENCILS

I always use a mechanical pencil for my initial line drawing. Because the lines are so light, unlike ordinary drawing pencils, they are easily removed with the kneaded eraser. As you work, replace the graphite lines with color.

CRAFT KNIVES

Craft knives are not just for cutting things; they can actually be used as drawing tools. When using Prismacolor, I use the edge of the knife to gently scrape away color to create texture such as hair or fur. A knife can also be used to remove unwanted specks that may appear in your work. As you can probably imagine, it is important to take care with this approach to avoid damaging the paper surface.

Erasers

Craft Knife

ACETATE GRAPHS

Acetate graphs are overlays to place over your photo reference. They have grid patterns on them that divide your picture into even increments, making it easier to draw accurately. I use them in both 1-inch (3cm) and ½-inch (1cm) divisions. They can be easily made by using a permanent marker on an acetate report cover. You can also draw one on paper and have it copied to a transparency on a copy machine.

TEMPLATES

Templates are stencils that are used to obtain perfect circles in your drawing. I use templates to draw pupils and irises on eyes for portraits and to make tires look accurate.

HORSEHAIR DRAFTING BRUSH

This is an essential tool when you are drawing, but even more so when using colored pencil. Colored pencil, particularly Prismacolor, will leave specks of debris as you work. Left on the paper, they can create nasty smudges that are hard to erase later. Brushing them with your hand can make it worse, and blowing them off will create moisture on your paper, which will leave spots. A drafting brush gently cleans your work area without smudging your art.

MAGAZINES

The best source for drawing material is magazines. I tear out pictures of many subjects and categorize them into different bins for easy reference. When you are learning to draw, magazines can provide a wealth of subject matter. When drawing people, there is nothing better than glamour magazines.

FIXATIVES

The type of spray that you use to fix your drawing depends again on the look you want your piece to ultimately have. I use two different types of finishing sprays, each one with its own characteristics.

The most common of the sprays, the workable fixative is undetectable when applied. The term "workable" means that you can continue drawing after you have applied the spray. Experience has taught me, however, that this is more true for graphite and charcoal than it is for colored pencil. I have found fixative to actually behave as a resist. I use it whenever I don't want the appearance of my work to change. When using Prismacolor, the wax of the pencil will rise to the surface, making the colors appear cloudy and dull. Workable fixative will stop this "blooming" effect and make the colors true again.

I use damar varnish when I want a high-gloss shine applied to my Prismacolor drawings. It will give the drawing the look of an oil painting and make the colors seem shiny and vivid. (Its primary use is to seal oil paintings.) I will often use this when drawing fruit and flowers, but it will also make a portrait beautiful.

Templates

Templates are helpful tools for drawing circles and ellipses for elements like tires. You can buy several variations of these plastic stencils. The ellipse template has shapes ranging from an almost complete circle to a very condensed, flat oval. These tools help you draw the outline of your shapes more accurately.

Chapter Two

DRAWING TECHNIQUES

Applying Tone

To create the types of drawings in this book, it's important to learn to use pencils properly. When teaching colored pencil techniques, I like to start students out with Verithin pencils to learn the layering technique. This approach allows the beginner to get the feel of applying colored pencil to the paper in an even layer. Erratic pencil strokes create an uneven, choppy appearance that looks amateur.

HOLDING THE PENCIL

A colored pencil has a "feel" to it. When drawing darker areas, I have a tendency to hold the pencil closer to the tip so I can apply more pressure without breaking the lead. As I move to lighter areas, I pull back, holding the pencil at a point farther from the tip. This helps me control the weight of the application for a softer approach and appearance.

LAYERING

Practice layering with value scales. Start applying an even, dark tone, with a sharp pencil and as you move over, apply lighter pressure to make a lighter tone. The more you practice, the more proficient you'll become. Start with black or another dark color to get the feel of applying pencil to paper.

It's important that the pencil lines are very close together and fill the area you're covering. You don't want to see little light spaces. Apply the pencil lines up and down, going back and forth slowly.

Squint your eyes periodically as you fade from dark to light; it helps you see how even your tones are. If you left little light areas, or hot spots as I call them, you can gently fill them in with a sharp pencil point. Allow your tones to gently fade into the color of the paper.

BURNISHING

Once you're comfortable with layering using Verithin pencils, try your hand with Prismacolor pencils. You'll see right away how different they are. When drawing a value scale with Verithin pencils, you used different pressures to get lighter or darker tones. Drawing with Prismacolor pencils involves applying different colors, blending each one into the others to change the tone. You may have to repeat the process a few or several times, reapplying colors as you go, to get the look you want.

Begin with three Prismacolor pencils—Black, White and Cool Gray 50%—to make a simple value scale. Again, apply the pencil evenly, but rather than letting the tone fade until it blends into the paper, use different colors for different light or dark tones. Continue to build layers until the colors cover the paper surface. To make the tones blend together, use firm pressure to apply a light color over a darker one. The colors will blend together, making the pigment look like paint. This painted look is perfect for drawing vehicles and capturing the reflective nature of cars.

Unlike layering with Verithin pencils, burnishing is better done with a fairly dull point. Practice is everything! These techniques do take time and patience, so give it the time it needs!

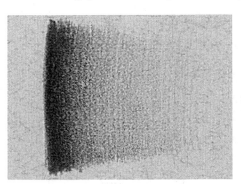

Layer With Verithin Pencils
Layer your colors very gradually as they fade from dark to light, altering your pressure as you go. There should be no choppiness between tones and no definitive line where one tone ends and another begins.

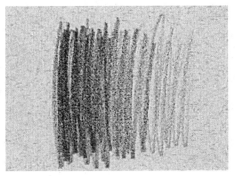

Use a Sharp Pencil for Layering
Layering is the process of using a very sharp pencil point and applying the tone evenly and gradually. DO NOT allow the pencil point to become dull. This alters the width of the pencil lead and makes the drawing look like you scribbled with crayons.

Burnish With Prismacolor Pencils
Apply an even layer of Black. Then overlap it with Cool Gray 50%. The two colors will blend together. Next apply a layer of White overlapping the gray. Continue burnishing, applying a dark color and overlapping it with a lighter one until they blend together for the smooth, gradual look you want.

Applying Color

Because the vehicles of NASCAR are so brightly colored, you should practice drawing some value scales using full color, too. Knowing how to use color for visual impact is important. Leaf through the book and look at the different drawings to see how I used color to create interest and contrast.

A good understanding of colors and how they work is essential to drawing with colored pencils. It all begins with the color wheel, which illustrates how colors relate to one another.

The basic groups of colors are primary and secondary colors. You can also sort colors into warm and cool colors or into pairs of complementary colors. Within each of these classifications, you will encounter shades and tints.

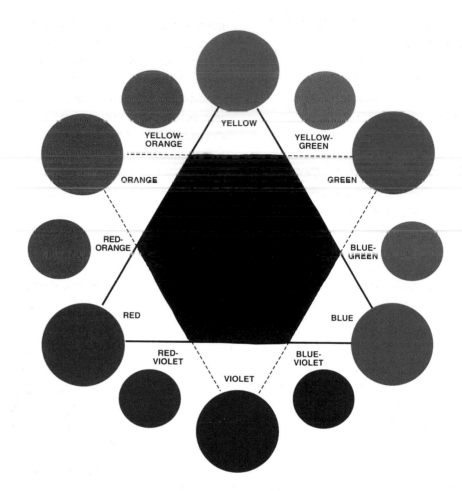

The Color Wheel

There are three primary colors: red, yellow and blue. These are pure colors and cannot be created by mixing other colors together. But mixing the primary colors in different combinations creates all the other colors. Mixing two primary colors together makes a secondary color. For instance, red mixed with yellow makes orange. You can see that a secondary color can be found on the color wheel between the two primary colors that created it.

WARM AND COOL COLORS

Warm colors fall on the yellow-orange-red side of the color wheel. Cool colors fall on the green-blue-violet side. Generally, warm colors jump out while cool colors seem more subdued.

COMPLEMENTARY COLORS

Complementary colors complement each other, or work well together. You can use them for many different purposes. For example, mixing complementary colors produces a gray or brown. To create shadows, it's always better to mix a color with its complement than to add black.

Complementary colors also can help each other stand out. For instance, to make the color red stand out, place green next to it. When drawing NASCAR cars and uniforms, you'll want to stay pretty true to life, but you can use complementary colors in the background or foreground.

SHADES AND TINTS

Shades and tints are important elements of color. A shade is a darker version of a color. A tint, on the other hand, is a lighter version. Shades and tints are the result of light and shadow: to shade a color, add another color to darken it; to create a tint, add a lighter color, like white.

HUE AND INTENSITY

Hue is color applied lightly; intensity is color applied brightly. Shades and tints are created by adding other colors; hue and intensity are achieved by using more or less of the color.

Warm Colors
Here's a value scale made up of the warm colors: yellow, yellow-orange, orange, red-orange, red and red-violet. I drew it with red, yellow and orange pencils and burnished it to create the in-between secondary colors.

Cool Colors
Here's a value scale made with the cool colors: violet, blue and green. Again, blending those three colors together created the secondary colors blue-violet and blue-green.

Complementary Colors
I drew this value scale with the complementary colors blue and orange. Complementary colors always appear opposite each other on the color wheel. When mixed, complements become gray or brown.

Hue and Intensity
Hue and intensity refer to the amount of a color that you've applied. In this case, I've applied just a little purple on the right to create a hue of purple. On the left I applied a lot of purple to create an intense purple.

Shades and Tints
You can see shades (darker versions of a color) and tints (lighter versions) on this value scale of the color red. The middle section is the true color. Everything on the left is a shade of red, created by adding another color. Everything on the right is a tint of red, created by adding white.

Shading and Form

Because it's important to fully understand what it takes to create depth and realism in your work, I always share with my students the five elements of shading and include practice exercises of the sphere.

Study the lit and shaded parts of basic shapes like the sphere.

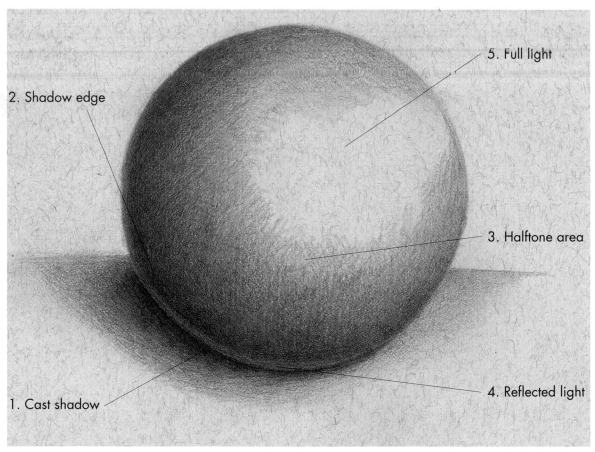

5. Full light

2. Shadow edge

3. Halftone area

4. Reflected light

1. Cast shadow

The Elements of a Sphere
These five elements can be found in every three-dimensional shape:

1. Cast Shadow: This is the darkest part of your drawing. It's just underneath the sphere where no light can reach. It gradually gets lighter as it moves away from the sphere.

2. Shadow Edge: This is where the sphere curves and the rounded surface begins to move away from the light.

3. Halftone Area: This is the true color of the sphere, unaffected by either shadows or strong light. It's located between the shadow edge and the full light area.

4. Reflected Light: This is the light edge along the rim of the sphere where it meets the surface on which the sphere is sitting. It indicates that light is reflecting off the surface or ground back onto the object. It's the most important element to include to illustrate the roundness of the surface.

5. Full Light: This is where the light is hitting the sphere at its strongest point.

Drawing a Sphere

Learning to draw a realistic sphere will help you with anything you want to draw. Practice drawing the sphere with this step-by-step example, using Verithin pencils. Remember the layering technique we practiced. Try to commit to memory the five elements of shading and form on a sphere.

For more practice, try drawing the sphere a few times in a few different colors. The more you practice this now, the better your drawings will be later. You can even practice drawing a sphere whenever you have some spare time. The practice will pay off.

COLORS USED

Verithin. Violet, Yellow Ochre.

1 Draw Outline

Begin your drawing with a light outline of a circle. Place a cast shadow underneath the circle on the left side. This is opposite the light source, which will be on the right.

2 Add Main Shadow

Apply the shadow edge inside and parallel to the rim of the sphere. Leave an area between the rim and the edge of this shadow to indicate reflected light. Lightly continue the tone up toward the full light area, lightening the color as you go.

3 Add Gradual Tone

Continue adding tone until the sphere looks like this. Smooth application of your pencil lines is essential for creating this look.

Drawing a Cylinder

Practice drawing a cylinder with Prismacolor pencils. Remember, you must use firmer pressure with these pencils to burnish, or blend the colors together. This gives the drawing more of a painted, filled in appearance.

Look at how different the five elements of shading appear on the cylinder. Whatever shape you're drawing, look and identify where the light source is, and find the five elements of shading.

COLORS USED

Prismacolor. Beige, Dark Brown, Light Umber, White.

1 Sketch Outline
Lightly sketch the shape of the cylinder with a mechanical pencil. Apply the cast shadow with Dark Brown. Soften the edge as it comes away from the cylinder by burnishing with Light Umber and then Beige. Use the lighter colors to soften the tones together.

2 Draw Shadow Edges
Apply the shadow edges with Dark Brown. Lighten your touch as you move to the halftone area. Overlap the Dark Brown with Light Umber, using the lighter color to blend the two together. Again, lighten your touch as you fade into the full light area.

3 Add Full Light Area
Fill in the full light area with Beige and White, blending the Beige into the Light Umber and then the White into the Beige.

Basic Shapes of NASCAR

To draw realistically, one of the most important things to accurately draw is the overall shape of an object. If the basic shape is off, the whole drawing just won't seem right. Think of each object you're drawing in terms of its basic shape, the foundation for the details you'll add to it.

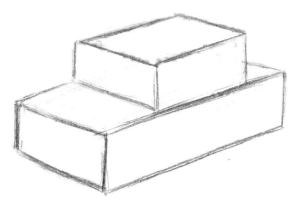

Cubes

The basic shape of a vehicle is like a cube in that it has a top, a bottom and four sides. The edges and angles separate all the surfaces.

Cubes in Vehicles

A car is like two cubes stacked together.

Cylinders

You can also see a cylinder in cars that have rounded bodies. You also can think of a cylinder as a rounded cube. Notice how the body style of the car at right resembles a cylinder.

Cylinders on Vehicles

In addition to the cylindrical shape of the cab of this car, certain elements also follow the principles of shading on a sphere. Look for the sphere shape on this car's fender.

Spheres

The sphere is also important when drawing other elements of NASCAR, such as helmets.

Sphere in a Helmet

Look at the upper edge of this helmet to see a bright glow of reflected light, just as on a sphere. You'll see helmets everywhere you go in NASCAR. This one belongs to a fireman assigned to one of the pit stalls.

The Breakdown of a NASCAR Vehicle

This is what NASCAR vehicles look like in basic shapes. You can see the way all four sides of the car are illustrated. Older cars were much boxier in shape; look at the old Earnhardt (page 15) and Petty (page 16) cars. Even with the modern body style, you can still see the basic shapes of the cubes clearly.

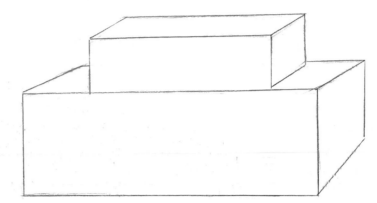

The Foundation Shapes
The shape of a car looks like two stacked cubes.

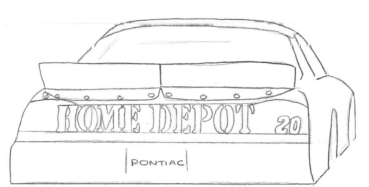

Translating Shapes Into a Line Drawing
You can clearly see the cube shapes in this line drawing of Tony Stewart's car.

Translating Shapes Into a Line Drawing
When you think of today's NASCAR vehicles, you probably picture sleek, aerodynamic cars. Now that you've seen how to get from the foundation cube shapes to the sleek look, you can still see the cubes in Tony's car.

NASCAR Winston Cup Specifications

Each area of a NASCAR vehicle has specific terminology. NASCAR vehicles must follow guidelines of weight and structure and have certain parts and no unauthorized ones.

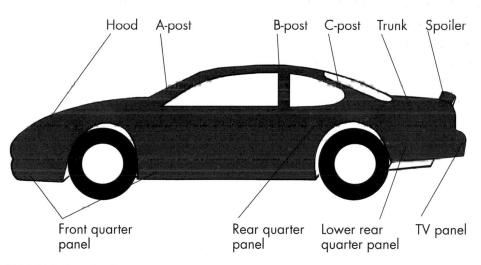

Hood   A-post   B-post   C-post   Trunk   Spoiler

Front quarter panel   Rear quarter panel   Lower rear quarter panel   TV panel

NASCAR Terminology

Above you'll see the terminology for different parts of a NASCAR vehicle.

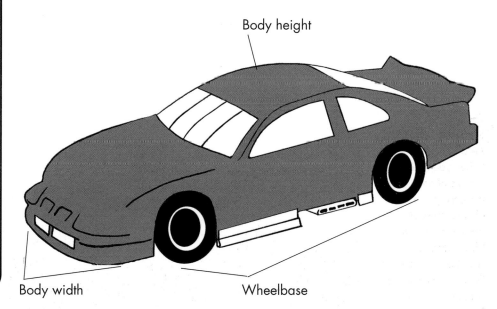

Body height

Body width   Wheelbase

NASCAR Guidelines

A NASCAR vehicle must weigh 3,400 pounds (1,530kg) without the driver. It must have a 110-inch (279cm) wheelbase, a 72½-inch (184cm) wide body and a 750 horsepower engine. Each car must be at least 51 inches (130cm) high.

Chapter Three

DRAWING TIRES, NUMBERS AND DECALS

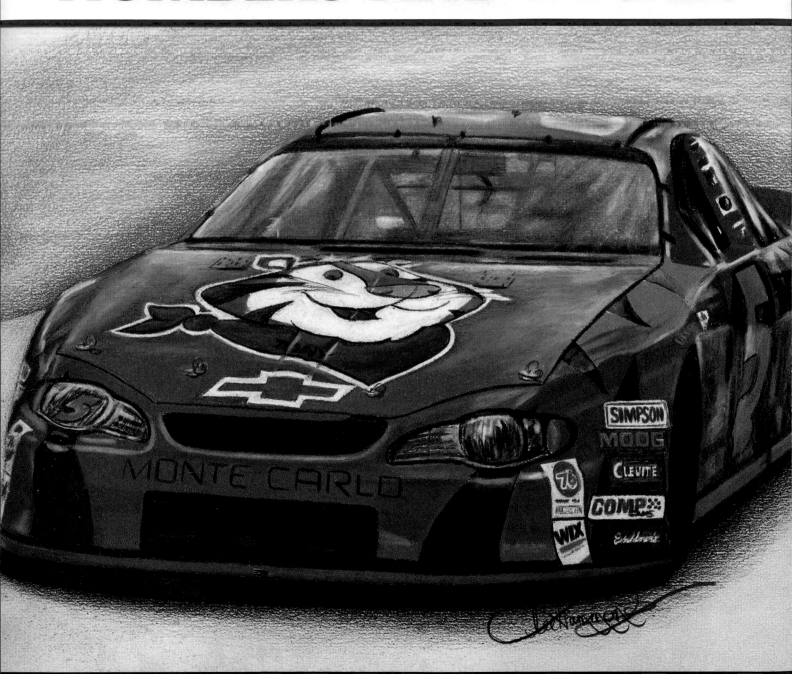

Perspective

Perspective is defined as the way a shape is perceived by the eye depending on the angle at which it is viewed. A circle is not a circle when viewed from the side; it's more condensed, like an oval. In racing, everything is moving, coming and going. Rarely will you will see anything still from a straight-on perspective.

Rows Show Perspective

Lines along the edges of the row of tires show how distance affects the appearance of a circle. We know in our minds that the tires are all the same size, but perspective makes them look otherwise. Each tire in this row appears smaller in both width and depth as the row recedes into the background.

If these lines were extended off the page, they'd eventually meet. The point where lines of perspective meet is called a vanishing point, and vanishing points always fall on the horizon line. Everything in the foreground of your drawing is drawn in relationship to the horizon line and the vanishing point or points on it.

NASCAR'S STORY

At the track, tires are laid out in rows for the teams to use during pit stops.

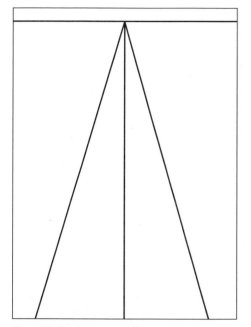

One-Point Perspective

Think of a highway that disappears into the distance, becoming smaller and narrower the farther away it gets. A highway—and a row of tires—both represent one-point perspective, in which the lines that extend from a shape converge at the same point on the horizon.

Indicating Distance With Size

Your mind knows that all of these cars are the same size, but you have to train your eyes to recognize that they actually appear smaller as they recede into the distance. The track, like the highway above, also gets smaller as it goes back.

Perspective on Tires

We all know that tires are round. And round things are circles, right? Well, what happens when you view a circular object from different angles? The change in appearance is dramatic.

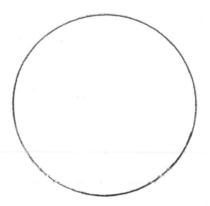

Standard Circle

This is a circle viewed straight on. This is the shape you think of when you think of a tire.

Standard Tire Shape

A tire is actually a circle only when viewed head on. Even the slightest change of perspective, or the viewpoint, will change the shape you see.

Vertical Ellipse

When viewed from a different angle, perhaps closer to a side view, the shape appears thinner than the full circle above. This is called an ellipse, which by definition is a circle in perspective.

The View From the Side

You can tell that this tire is heading away from you by its angle and the shape of the ellipse. The rounder the ellipse, the closer you're getting to returning to a front view.

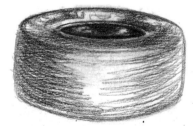

Horizontal Ellipse

This is a circle viewed from above. Instead of a thin appearance, like the vertical ellipse above, this ellipse seems flattened out.

The View From Above

You'd have this view of a tire that is lying a few feet away on the ground. Unless a car is wrecked and lying on its side, you'd see this perspective of a tire only when the tire is off of the car.

Drawing Tires

Drawing ellipses is not an easy process. It takes a lot of practice to make car tires look right. This exercise will help you gain some experience. I suggest using a mechanical pencil to practice. It's easier to erase so you can make corrections as you go. Colored pencil is not as forgiving and is harder to erase. After you've gained some experience, you can switch over to colored pencil.

When drawing ellipses, you must take time. There is a lot of psychology associated with drawing. Even though your eyes see the ellipse, your mind "sees" a circle. Don't get frustrated. You'll need a lot of discipline to not draw an overly round shape.

Templates are handy for drawing tires, but finding the right size and shape hole in the stencil can be difficult. Draw the general shape freehand first. Then you can more easily match a stencil to that shape and use it to clean up your drawing.

Sometimes the angle and size of the tires you're trying to draw will prevent you from finding the perfect ellipse from your templates. In this case, you can use French curve templates, which offer a variety of edges that you can line up with your drawing. They don't help you draw complete shapes, but they do at least help create clean edges.

When becoming proficient in drawing anything, it takes tons of

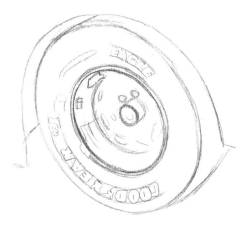

practice. After working on this exercise, take your favorite racing magazines and draw as many tires as possible from as many views as you can find.

1 Draw Basic Outline

The basic outline of a tire. This is the stage in which you need to be very accurate. Look closely at the distances between the edges of the tire and be careful not to draw the tire too round compared to your reference.

In addition to the general shape of the entire tire, study the combination of interlocking shapes that make up the tire. Notice all the geometric shapes that make up this wheel. Pay attention to where you place these shapes in your drawing, and compare their placements to other shapes in your drawing and to your photo reference. Again, your accuracy will improve with practice.

2 Begin Adding Tone

Begin placing the dark tones. Think about which areas will be lighter or even white. Consider each area you're shading as a geometric shape that interlocks with others to complete a puzzle. When all the different shaded areas are placed together, the final product resembles a realistic looking tire.

3 Finish the Puzzle

Layer the tone as needed to get a good range of darks and lights. Remember to continue to refer to your reference after you get your outline down on paper. The subtle color and value shifts are as important as the general shapes in drawing an accurate depiction.

Reference Photo
Use this photo of a tire as a guide.

Tire Scenes

In the garage area of a racetrack or around pit road, there are tires for as far as you can see. When taking reference photographs for this book, I was amazed at how interesting tires really are! The way they are stacked, placed and handled is a work of art in itself. As an artist, there is a lot to be learned by drawing them.

Vertical Cylinder
The stacked tires in this photo form an excellent cylindrical shape. Refer to page 28 to study the effects of shading on a cylinder and compare them to this cylinder. Any rounded object shows the effects of the five elements of shading.

Subtle Perspective
Study the tire perched on top. Notice how it's slightly turned. The tire no longer is in the shape of a circle. Now it's an ellipse. This variation in shape makes these tires a wonderful learning and drawing experience. I was careful to study all of the geometric shapes of the inside wheel, to assist me in getting the ellipse correct. Instead of using a template, I drew these tires freehand, visually measuring and comparing distances between the various shapes. You'll see this view of a tire often when drawing race cars.

Horizontal Cylinder
Placed side by side, tires resemble a horizontal cylinder.

Changing Tires

Like everything in NASCAR, tires follow certain guidelines. Tires are assigned to each team for every race, and each team has a tire specialist who monitors and analyzes the wear, pressure and temperature on the tires during each pit stop. The data the specialist collects helps the team adjust the suspension of the vehicle during the race.

Ready ...

Before a race, you'll see brightly colored pieces of tape on each tire. It's critical that the tire changer grabs the tire in the right place, and the tape tells him where to pick it up in order to avoid hitting the valve stem.

... Set ...

While the race is in progress, members of the pit crew select the tires they'll need for the next pit stop and rest them against the pit wall.

... Go

Dewayne Colvard, front tire carrier for Woods Brothers Racing Team, stands ready to jump the wall when he receives the signal. As the car comes in for service, the crew mounts the wall, prepared to jump over. It's not just the speed of the car that wins races. The pit crew has to turn over pit stops as quickly as possible. The tire carrier must place the tire strategically, ready to go over the wall with him.

Graphing

Being able to see shapes accurately and translate them onto paper is not easy. Freehand drawing is often fun and enjoyable, but it's rarely accurate, at least without a large time investment.

To teach how to draw shapes accurately, I use the graphing method. It's the easiest way I know to break down complicated shapes into more manageable pieces. To create my drawings I draw one-inch (3cm) squares over my reference photographs to form a grid. This makes the many details of the vehicles easier to capture.

While some artists argue that graphing or creating an outline with a projector is cheating, I couldn't disagree more. I teach my students to both graph and project images to train their eye to see shapes accurately. I am a self-taught artist, and this is one of the ways I honed my skills. I attribute my ability to draw

freehand with a high degree of accuracy to using the graph and projector repeatedly early in my training. This repetition of capturing shapes and seeing how one shape connects to another increases your ability to freehand accurately.

An opaque projector is a machine that uses a lightbulb to shine the image of a photograph down onto the surface of your drawing paper. Often in my classes, I check a student's freehand ability against the projector. I take the photograph the student is drawing from and place it in the projector to project that image over the student's freehand drawing. The inaccuracies in the drawing become apparent, and then the student can analyze where he or she went wrong and make the appropriate corrections.

Our ability to see shapes is due to our perception, how our brains have learned to see things. We often make

the same mistakes over and over without even realizing it. If we're seeing things inaccurately, the graph and projector force us to see things in a different way, as individual shapes, so we can learn to see them as they really are. The graph helps you see shapes accurately by dividing images into smaller, more manageable shapes.

DRAWING A GRID ON YOUR PHOTO

Draw a grid of one-inch (3cm) squares over the part of your photo that you want to include in your drawing. You can scan your photos on a computer or make color copies so that you don't have to draw directly on a photograph. When it's time to add color to your drawing, though, return to your original photo so you can refer to the most accurate colors possible.

Graphed Photo
This photograph of Kevin Harvick's #29 Goodwrench Chevrolet will be much easier to draw using the grid method. You can draw a similar grid on your drawing surface and then draw the shape in each box of the photo into the corresponding box on your paper. The placement of your shapes will be much more accurate.

DRAWING A GRID ON YOUR PAPER

I draw a grid on my paper or mat board so I can "translate" the image from the photo to the paper. If you want to draw an image larger than your photo, you can make the squares in your grid larger. If you want to draw a smaller image, you can make the squares in your grid smaller. As long as your grid is made of squares and is made of the same number of squares as the grid on your photo, the shapes you're drawing will be proportional to the shapes in the photo.

Make sure you draw the grid on your paper with extremely light lines. You'll need to erase the grid when you finish drawing the shapes of the car. I use a mechanical pencil and apply the graphite with a very light touch. The grids in this book are darker then they should be so you can see them. When I'm drawing on my own, my grids are so light that you can barely see them. Use a kneaded eraser to erase a grid. It will lift the lines without damaging the paper's surface.

Finished Drawing

This is what your drawing should look like when you're done. Never remove your grid until you're sure all your shapes are accurate. This is where you need to take your time. Remember, draw much lighter than what you see here, so you can make corrections with your kneaded eraser as you go. Don't use your typewriter eraser for corrections or for removing your grid lines. It is way too abrasive and will rough up your paper surface.

Graphed Drawing Surface

Study the graphed photograph on page 38. Look inside each of the squares. Each square contains shapes and by looking at those shapes and where they fit within the box, you can reproduce them in the grid drawn on your drawing paper. This is much easier than trying to determine where that little shape belongs within the entire drawing.

Start very slowly and draw lightly. Draw as accurately as possible; correct placement of shapes and lines within each square is essential for the squares to come together into a natural-looking drawing. As you move from square to square, make sure your shapes are connecting properly. For instance, the windshield of the car crosses over several squares. Draw each square separately, but stop every once in a while to make sure the lines of the windshield line up as they should.

Drawing Decals and Numbering

A NASCAR vehicle is an advertiser's dream come true—a rolling billboard! These cars sport many decals, each representing a company and sponsorship. A sponsor makes a team financially capable of racing a car. Whether a driver races at a local track or competes in the NASCAR series, a sponsor funds the team. In exchange, the team displays the company's decal on the car. The better the team and driver are, the more visibility and air time that car gets on TV; the higher the visibility, the more it costs to advertise on that car. Primary sponsors pay millions of dollars to secure high visibility placement on the car, such as on the hood or under the rear spoiler. Paint schemes also advertise the sponsors. For instance, Home Depot's bright orange and white colors are instantly recognizable on the #20 Chevrolet of Tony Stewart.

After each race, the car is refurbished and returned to its pristine state. All cars look "brand new" at the beginning of each race. Each team actually has several cars, including one to take on the track and one for backup. Because each track is made differently, the teams custom-build cars to run according to the needs and specifications of each track. Some are short tracks and some are super speedways. Some are relatively flat, while others have high degrees of "banking."

At the beginning of each season, the teams receive the sheets detailing the new paint scheme assigned to their vehicles. Sheets showing the matching uniforms and helmets are also provided. These sheets are also sent to all of the licensees (like me!) who market and sell NASCAR products. I use these official references to help with my illustrations.

Each year, the paint schemes are altered to reflect any changes in sponsorship. These can be small changes, like the placement of the decals or the addition of a new sponsor, but sometimes the changes can be quite drastic, like the acquisition of a new primary sponsor. (*That* requires a totally new paint scheme!) Part of the excitement of a new season is simply checking out the fresh designs on the cars as they roll past for the first time.

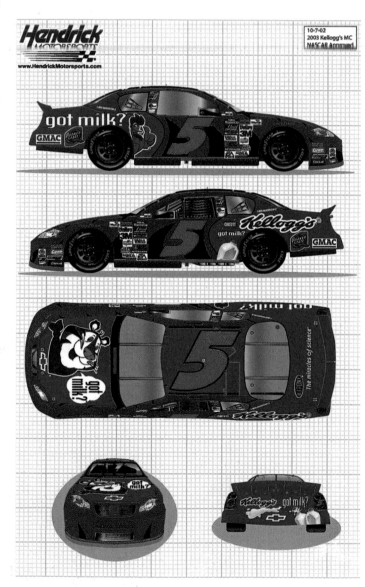

The Coming Season's Paint Scheme
Sheets like these are provided to the teams and licensees each time there are changes in paint schemes or sponsor decal placement.

40

Transportation

To get from track to track, the teams move the cars and equipment in large haulers. Like the NASCAR vehicles, they are prime advertising opportunities for the sponsors. Their company name, logo and characters are boldly displayed and rolled down the interstates and highways each week.

The sheets at right show the sponsors' decal placement on the haulers. Each area has very high visibility.

Inside the track, all the team haulers are lined up in rows (see middle photo).

Inside the haulers, you will find everything the team will need. A hauler is a two-story wonder, able to hold two entire race cars (stored in an overhead compartment) as well as extra engines, car parts, and all of the crew's tools and equipment. Everything is housed in special drawers and compartments. The hauler also has technical computer equipment for testing parts, an office area and driver lounge.

If the teams need "anything" it has to be transported in their hauler.

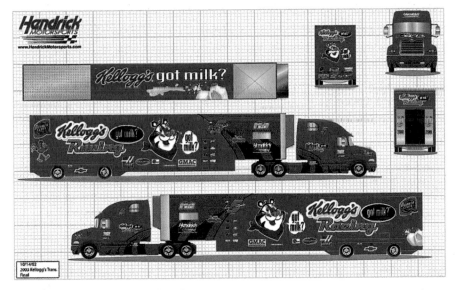

The Team Hauler's Look for the Season
These sheets show the placement of sponsor decals on the team hauler. The haulers also act as rolling billboards for the sponsors.

The Team Haulers
The haulers are lined up in rows in the garage area inside the track, ready to move the team, cars and equipment to the next track.

Inside a Hauler
Everything a team member could need to do his job is hauled from race to race.

Perspective on Decals

In drawing race cars, the most difficult aspect is drawing the numbers and letters of the decals correctly. The perspective of them changes, depending on the way the car is positioned. It is the same dilemma we encountered when drawing tires. When viewed at an angle, things no longer appear the way we view them straight on. I took these two drawings off my sheets for Terry Labonte's car with Hendrick Motorsports.

In the drawing on the left, the "Tony the Tiger" character is seen from above; everything appears straight on, so the perspective is normal. It is clear, and easy to read.

However, in the drawing on the right the car is coming forward so the image appears different. You can see the effects of perspective. Look at Tony the Tiger. In this view, he appears distorted and condensed. It's much like the principle we discussed when drawing tires. Tony has a circular shape. When seen at an angle, he takes on the ellipse characteristic.

Although both of these drawings look very pretty, they are more cartoon-like than realistic. Look on the following page to see what this car looks like captured in realistic rendering.

The Different Faces of "Tony the Tiger"
The vantage point on the left shows "Tony the Tiger" with no distortion because he is seen straight on. The picture on the right shows a different angle of perspective, one which condenses the figure and makes it more elliptical.

Reflection

Although the drawings on the previous page were fun to draw, they were taken from the designer sheets, and are not very realistic. They are drawn with solid colors, showing no effects of light and shadow. In reality, the reflective surface of a car contains many elements that change the appearance of the colors. These details need to be captured in your artwork for it to look real.

Check out this photo of Terry Labonte's car at the racetrack. Can you see how the shiny, reflective quality of the car changes the way everything looks? It was a bright, beautiful day, and the reflection of the sky and clouds can be seen on the front of the car. You can see the reflection of the clouds in the windshield and hood, and the side of the car appears very dark. The decals are no longer easy to read. It is this type of realism that will make your racing art more impressive.

Keep in mind that the lighting effects the colors of the car. The areas that are in bright sunlight appear lighter, whereas the colors in shadow appear darker. Study the effects of light and shadow on the orange. In the bright highlighted areas, the orange takes on a pinkish hue. In the shadow areas, the orange takes on a shade of red.

I captured these color changes with Prismacolor. With Prismacolor pencils and burnishing, you can add colors over and over, blending them together as you go. Using the lighter colors to burnish over the darker ones gives your artwork a realistic look.

You can't be timid with this technique! Have fun and add as much color as you want to capture the small shapes and patterns of the reflections. Look at the windshield to see how I created the patterns of light and dark. It gives the illusion of seeing the inside of the car combined with the reflection on the glass.

Terry Labonte's #5 Kellogg's Chevrolet at the Racetrack

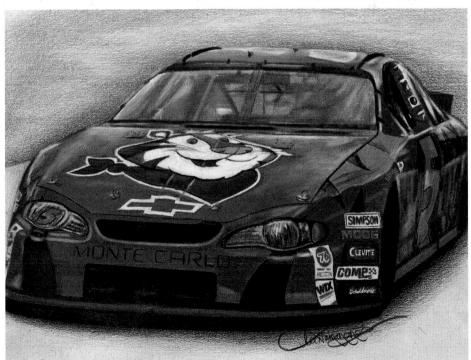

Color Captured With Prismacolor

The #5 Kellogg's Chevrolet driven by Terry Labonte
8" × 10" (20cm × 25cm)
Prismacolor pencils on no. 3297 Arctic White mat board

COLORS USED

Prismacolor. Poppy Red, Pale Vermillion, Canary Yellow, Periwinkle, Cloud Blue, Copenhagen Blue, Mediterranean Blue, Cool Gray 50%, Cool Gray 70%, Black, White.

Vantage Points

When drawing cars, you must learn to draw in perspective. These two photographs are taken from one of Jeff Gordon's old cars that are on display at the Hendrick Motorsports museum in Concord, North Carolina. From these two views, you can see how the angles affect the way the numbers and decals appear. Since NASCAR is all about the cars coming and going, learning how to draw these shots is essential if you are going to illustrate motor sports.

Both of these photos would be good practice pieces to draw from.

First Vantage Point
Not only can you see the heavily reflective quality of the car from this angle, but you can see the wide variety of sponsors' decals on the #24 car. Check out Jeff Gordon's autograph right above the window and draw it as you see it.

Second Vantage Point
Some decals change on the driver's side of the car, others remain the same. The reflective quality on this side is interesting, too; see how the showroom floor is reflected along the bottom?

The Paint Job After the Race

Donuts the NASCAR Way

Have you ever heard of a "donut?" I'm not talking about what we eat for breakfast or even turning a car in tight circles in a parking lot. A "donut" in racing refers to the black, circular shape rubbed into the side of a race car by another driver racing at your side. It is hard to imagine rubbing against another car at 200 miles per hour, but it happens regularly, and takes the paint right off the car.

Swapping Paint

Sometimes when passing or being passed, race cars scrape up against one another, leaving behind a long area of roughed-up paint on the cars. This is where the term "swapping paint" comes from. These beautiful paint jobs really take a beating!

As bad as this looks, by the next week, a brand new paint job (or car) rolls on to the track for a fresh start!

Draw the #12

Sometimes the numbers on the cars are fairly simple. The #12 off of Ryan Newman's Alltel Ford is not difficult to draw.

However, the lines follow the contours of the car, and are not as straight as you may think. They have a slight curve to them, which is very important. This exercise will give you some practice.

> **COLORS USED**
>
> *Prismacolor.* White, Cloud Blue, True Blue, Black.

Graphed Reference Photo

1 Draw the Number

When drawing this number, take note of how the lines gently curve to conform to the rounded shape of the car door.

You will notice an upside-down arrow below the 12. You will see this on all cars below the number, and centered on the vehicle. This is called a "jack point." This arrow indicates to the "jack man" (the crew member in charge of hoisting the car during a pit stop) where the point of the jack is to be inserted.

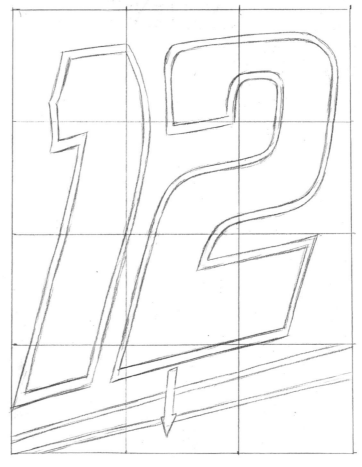

2 Add the Color

When applying Prismacolor, it is important to always apply the lightest color first. This keeps the darker colors from smearing into lighter colors as you work. In this case, the white needs to be applied first. However, when analyzing the white area in the photo, you can see that it isn't a flat white color. Because of the curve of the car, the lower area of the 12 is actually a pale shade of gray.

Cover the entire area of the number with White Prismacolor first. This gives you a foundation to build on. For the slight gray color, use Cloud Blue. The white reflects the blue color surrounding it, making Cloud Blue more accurate. Apply the Cloud Blue over the white and then use the white to burnish the two colors together. The tonal change is subtle, but helps the look of realism.

Finishing the drawing is really just a matter of filling in the blue edge of the number with True Blue Prismacolor and the rest of the surrounding area with Black. Whenever you are working with Prismacolor pencils, it is very important to spray the drawing when you are finished. The wax content of these pencils rises to the surface of your drawing and makes it look "milky." Spraying it with a workable fixative when you are finished takes this dullness away and makes the colors look deeper.

Draw the #10

Each car has its own unique look, depending on the artist and designer in charge of the paint scheme. Some of the driver numbers are quite unusual. I thought this number 10, which is on the #10 Valvoline Pontiac of Johnny Benson, would make an interesting step-by-step project.

Use the graph that has been applied to the number 10 to get the basic shapes. Be careful! Even though this looks simple, it is easy to get lost while drawing the outline in regular pencil. Since this number is outlined with three colors (blue, yellow and black), accurately outlining in graphite alone can be difficult.

I used my pencil to "fill in" the area that will be blue so I don't have so many lines to figure out.

> **COLORS USED**
>
> *Prismacolor.* French Gray 10%, White, Canary Yellow, Peacock Blue, Black.

Graphed Reference Photo

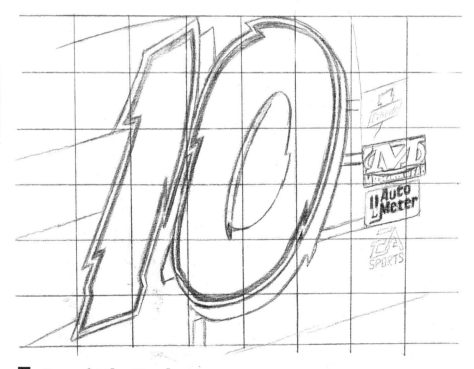

1 Draw in the Numbers

Use the graph as a guide as you draw. With your pencil, fill in the outline areas that will be blue. This will keep you from getting lost as you draw. Having too many lines is very confusing!

Try your hand at some of the decals and their lettering. This is a good way to familiarize yourself with some of the sponsor decals that you will see over and over on the various race cars.

2 Apply Lightest Colors First

As we learned in the previous example with the #12, it is important to always apply the lightest color in your drawing first. In this case, the number needs to be filled in first. At first glance, this number appears to be white. However, if you look closely, you will see where the ridge along the door panel is slightly lighter in color. This means that the number is actually "darker" than white. I used French Gray 10% for the entire number, and then applied White for the ridge area.

Lighten your graphite lines before you apply the light colors. Graphite smears easily and will get into your color and make it look dirty. When colored pencil is applied over graphite, the graphite lines become extremely dark and permanent.

I used Canary Yellow to fill in the yellow areas. Again, be careful to lighten your graphite to prevent smearing.

3 Complete With Dark Colors

Complete your work by filling in the blue area with Peacock Blue. In the area where the door ridge protrudes, add a little White over it for a highlight effect. Then add Black around the edge of the number and into the shadow shapes.

If you have chosen to practice working on some of the sponsor decals, I suggest switching to the Verithin pencils. They have sharper points which are better for creating thin lines.

Draw the #6

This number is not very difficult to draw either, not when using the grid method for placement. Use the boxes to guide you. The white area of the 6 looks even, without the affects of a shadow. I chose to leave the white of the paper for this area, to avoid smearing. To keep an area like this clean as you work, you can use the typewriter eraser. It is abrasive enough to remove stubborn colored pencil flakes if they get stuck here.

The paint scheme of Mark Martin's #6 Viagra Ford has beautiful striping. The grid method helps you draw them accurately and in the right place.

Graphed Reference Photo

COLORS USED

Prismacolor. Non-Photo Blue, Peacock Blue, True Blue, Deco Yellow, Cool Gray 70%, Black.

1 Draw the Number

After removing the graph from your drawing, redraw any lines that were accidentally erased and clean up your edges with your eraser. Make sure your shapes are accurate before you begin to add color.

2 Apply the Lightest Colors

Once you are sure your lines are accurate, start by applying the lightest colors first. Use Non-Photo Blue for the lightest blue stripes. These stripes are lighter "above" the 6, and become darker below. For the lower area, switch to True Blue.

The blue area surrounding the 6 changes colors, too. Study where it is light and where it is darker. Use Peacock Blue for the darker stripes.

Leave the white area of the 6 open. Keep this area clean with a typewriter eraser as you work. Fill in the letters on the tire with Deco Yellow.

3 Add the Darker Colors

Continue with all the various shades of blue and then add Black. Black goes into the shadow behind the 6, in the wheel well, and into the large stripe.

The large black stripe is altered by a reflective highlight. Go back to the reference photo and study it. You can see the reflection there. Part of this stripe needs to be filled in with Cool Gray 70%.

In the wheel well, you can see how the inside is dark above the tire and then becomes lighter as it reaches the bottom. Use Black and the two shades of gray to graduate the tones.

Use a sharp point on your Black pencil to carefully outline the letters on the tires.

Specialty Paint Schemes

These are two examples of what special promotion paint schemes can look like.

This #3 Goodwrench Chevrolet looks nothing like the typical jet black vehicle that Dale Earnhardt was known for. Peter Max, a pop artist known for his wild colors and psychedelic designs, created this car for Earnhardt. He drove this car in May of 2000 at two separate events—the Winston and the Coca Cola 600, both at Lowes Motor Speedway.

Most specialty paint schemes such as this are made for specific appearances, and are only driven once or twice.

This #88 UPS Ford was a special paint scheme driven by Dale Jarrett in September of 2001. It was for the inaugural race at the opening of the Kansas Speedway.

The #3 Goodwrench Chevrolet ... In Color
It's a shock to see the normally all-black Goodwrench Chevrolet with so much color. The paint scheme was created specially by pop artist Peter Max.

The Specially Painted #88 UPS Ford
Because Jarrett's sponsor is UPS, this paint scheme was also seen on the UPS delivery trucks.

Using Color to Draw Interest

When drawing the cars of NASCAR, adding creativity of your own will make your work more dynamic. In each of these examples I have chosen to incorporate the driver's name into the background of the drawing for more interest. I think it creates a wonderful design, and makes the artwork fun and colorful.

In this drawing of Tony Stewart's Home Depot Pontiac, I used color to make it more interesting. The cool lavender color of the paper makes the bright orange stand out in contrast. By repeating the orange around the lettering, and even into the shadow area under the car, the entire drawing comes together. By lightly shading the inside of the letters with black, the letters take on a three-dimensional quality.

I made the letters in the drawing of Jeff Gordon's DuPont Chevrolet a bit more colorful, to match the bright paint scheme. By using a yellow paper, the whole drawing seems to glow with color. The checkerboard floor gives the illusion of being in "Victory Lane." This drawing is the final step to the project presented on page 78.

Tony Stewart's #20 Home Depot Pontiac
Contrasting cool and warm colors makes this drawing interesting. Adding the lettering behind the car adds excitement.

Jeff Gordon's #24 DuPont Chevrolet
Color contrasting makes the bright color of the car stand out.

Create Your Own NASCAR Paint Scheme

Have you ever wondered what it would be like to create your own paint design for a NASCAR vehicle? The sky is the limit to what can be placed on these cars, and designing them can be fun. When studying paint schemes, you will see all kinds. They range from elaborate, highly decorative ones, with brilliant colors, to the more solid colors with nothing but lettering adorning them.

Using this "blank" car as a foundation, see what you can design. All race car paint schemes have a "theme," or a logo they are trying to display. You can use whatever you want on your design. Think of what you might like based on your favorite colors and your favorite number.

I have sketched out a basic design for a "LeeHammond.Com" Car. My favorite number is 57, so I've used that as a start. I also placed my signature and company name on the deck lid and on the side. From that point on, the color will create the total "look." Sometimes drawings like these are better when they aren't over-planned. I will let my creativity flow as I start the color rendering.

1 Use the Blank Car to Start Your Own Design

Use this blank car to design your own NASCAR vehicle paint scheme. If it helps, make a copy of the car and place a graph over it to get the proportions accurate. You could also have the drawing enlarged to make it easier to draw.

2 Draw in Details Before Color

Use things like your favorite number, colors and patterns for your design. Much of the creativity will come when applying color.

3 Complete Your Car

This is the finished LeeHammond.Com car. It has all the elements I would want in a NASCAR vehicle of my own. Even though it is very bright and dynamic looking, the rendering was done in only four colors.

Give the drawing impact by including the finish line in the front and by drawing "speed streaks" in the back. More use of the illusion of speed will be in chapter six.

The Official LeeHammond.Com Car
12" x 16" (30cm x 41cm)
Prismacolor pencils on no. 8297 Arctic White mat board

Chapter Four

DRAWING THE CAR

Rendering Realistically

When you look at realistic rendering such as the drawings in this book, you can see how many elements need to come together in order for the look to be created. As we learned in previous chapters, the foundation of the entire drawing is in the basic outline and accurate shapes. Those have to be done first.

When creating your personal race car on pages 54 and 55, there was a huge difference between the outline version and the finished artwork. Now that you have learned how to achieve accuracy in your shapes with the use of a graph, it is time to learn the rendering phase.

Catching Subjects
Here I am photographing the NASCAR Craftsman Truck race at the I-70 Speedway in Kansas City. The truck races are some of my favorites—you never know what to expect!

NASCAR Craftsman Truck Series
Mike Bliss, driving for the Xpress Motorsports team in his #16 Chevy truck, took the 2002 NASCAR Craftsman Truck Series Championship.

9" x 12" (23cm x 31cm)
Prismacolor and Verithin pencils on no. 3305 English Stone mat board

NASCAR'S STORY

The NASCAR Craftsman Truck Series is one of the most exciting series of the sport. While the performance and the mechanics of the vehicles are similar, the trucks are known for a bit more "bumping and rubbing" on the track.

COLORS USED

Verithin. (Truck) Black, Poppy Red, Crimson Red, Tuscan Red, Canary Yellow, White, Clay Rose, Sunburst Yellow, Ultramarine Blue, Neon Yellow.

Prismacolor. (Background) Black, True Blue, True Green.

#29—Kevin Harvick

Let's complete the line drawing we started on page 59 of Kevin Harvick's #29 GM Goodwrench Chevrolet. We'll use Verithin pencils on no. 3297 Arctic White mat board.

COLORS USED

Verithin. Black, True Blue, Carmine Red, Scarlet Red, Ultramarine Blue, Orange, Canary Yellow.

Prismacolor. Black, White, Poppy Red.

Reference Photo

Graphed Reference Photo
Kevin Harvick's #29 GM Goodwrench Chevrolet. Study this photo for the light source before you begin to draw.

1 Erase the Graph Lines

It is important to take great care when removing the grid lines from your drawing paper. DO NOT use the typewriter eraser to remove these lines. It is abrasive and will damage the paper, leaving rough areas that cannot be hidden later. Always use your kneaded eraser to remove the grid lines. Roll it into a point with your fingers and gently stroke the line until it disappears. It is not hard to see why drawing the graph line lightly on your paper in the beginning is important!

Take great care when removing the graph that you don't **erase** your car shapes with it. Go slowly and redraw things as you go. When the graph is finally gone, this is what your drawing will look like.

2 Secure Shapes

Look for the light source in any subject first. Here, the silver paint with the bright sunlight creates highlighted areas that are quite intense. Even though the lettering on the deck lid is black, the lighting makes it seem pale and gray in color.

To begin rendering, start with the dark areas. Apply the shadow area around the right side of the hood with a very sharp Black Verithin pencil. Also fill in the vent and grill in the front. Shading in the dark area under the car will help separate it from the foreground. At this stage, the car is already taking shape.

Look at the reference photo again. Can you see how light the top of the car is? To draw something that is very light in color when working on white paper, you must create an edge, usually by placing tone into the background area. With your Black Verithin and a light touch, gently add some tone along the edges of the car to give it the illusion of being a light car against a darker background. This technique also gives the drawing the look of distance. Apply a few dark areas into the windshield area.

3 Bring in Color

With the True Blue Verithin, layer some color over the black that has already been applied. Notice how the colors layer on top of one another without building up. Keeping a sharp point on the pencil is essential to keep the edges sharp and tones consistent. If necessary, practice a few value scales using the Black and True Blue before you begin.

With Ultramarine Blue Verithin, add the GM logo to the middle of the hood below the windshield. Apply this color lightly; the bright highlights of the sun make this look pale.

With Carmine Red Verithin, place the Chevrolet logo on the front of the hood. Apply the red stripe around the bottom edge of the car with Poppy Red Prismacolor pencil. This area isn't washed out by the highlight, so the color appears much more intense. This is a good situation for switching to Prismacolor.

With the black and red pencils, you've applied an abstract area of color on the right side of the car. This is where the perspective and angle of the car has distorted all of the lettering, making it appear as a "blob." When working on areas like this, refer to the photograph and study the effects of the light and shadow. Look at everything as "nonsense shapes" and draw those as that instead of what they really are. Thinking of them that way helps you draw what you see rather than what you know.

KEVIN HARVICK

2001 Raybestos Rookie of the Year

Kevin Harvick drives for Richard Childress Racing. A versatile driver, Harvick has won races in the NASCAR Featherlite Modified Series, NASCAR Busch Series, NASCAR Craftsman Truck Series, as well as the NASCAR Winston Cup. After the death of Dale Earnhardt, he took over the GM Goodwrench Chevrolet ride.

14" × 17" (36cm × 43cm)
Graphite on 2-ply

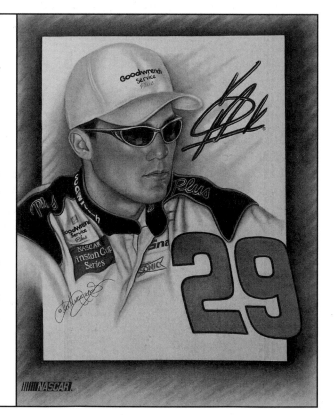

4 Add the Finishing Touches

Add a slight hint of Scarlet Red with the Verithin pencil to warm up the tones and create contrast. Sometimes a little deviation from reality can help the drawing look better.

To smooth out the tones and help with the reflective look, use the White Prismacolor pencil to burnish over the car. Lightly go over the entire hood, the windshield and the side of the car. This helps dull the tones and color, making the sunlight effect even more obvious. The front of the car has been left alone, so those details are crisper in nature.

Work on the details of the decals, trying to be as accurate as possible on this scale. Sometimes, I use the very sharp edge of a craft knife to create edges and lines in the lettering. You can gently scrape lines into areas that are too thin to either draw with a pencil or remove with an eraser.

With a straightedge, create a wall behind the car and add a line on the pavement that recedes. Simple things like these can add a lot to a drawing. Notice the perspective again, how these lines seem to be converging into a "V" as they recede into the right side of the paper.

The background is one of the most important elements of this drawing. It is the darkness of the background that makes the car stand out and look brightly lit in comparison. The darkness helps define the light edges of the car.

#12—Ryan Newman

When drawing the vehicles of NASCAR, it is important to know how to draw all the views. This is the #12 Alltel Ford of Ryan Newman as seen from the side/rear perspective. Using the grid method makes this type of angle much easier to draw.

Be sure to take a lot of time when drawing the numbers and letters on the car. For instance, look at how different the word Alltel looks on the side of the car when compared to the rear. This is another perfect example of perspective and how things look different from various angles and vantage points.

This is where the boxes of the graph will really help you with placement. Remember to draw lightly as you go and make corrections along the way. Draw what you see one box at a time. Don't move to another box until everything is accurate.

COLORS USED

Verithin. Black, Indigo Blue, True Blue, Pale Vermillion, Crimson Red, Violet.

Prismacolor. Canary Yellow.

Reference Photo

Graphed Reference Photo

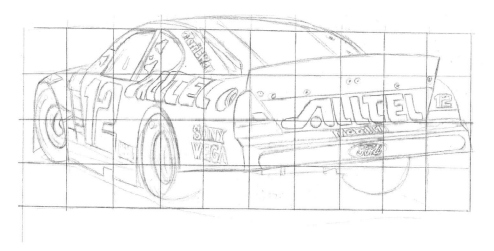

1 Use the Graph to Draw

Before you begin, study the reference photo. Look for key elements that need to be included in your drawing or for any small things that could be eliminated, like unnecessary background.

Make sure that all the details and shapes of the car are drawn In correctly. Accuracy at this stage is essential, so go from box to box, checking carefully for accuracy. Pay special attention to the numbers and letters and how perspective changes their appearance. Take your time with this; it will pay off later.

Gently remove the graph lines with your kneaded eraser. Reapply any lines that may disappear in the process.

2 Secure Shapes

Once the graph lines are removed, the first thing to do is clean up the edges and secure shapes. Outline all the lettering with a Black Verithin pencil. Take your time to make sure all the edges are straight, even, and in proportion. For the Alltel on the back of the car, use a straightedge. Everything else can be drawn freehand.

3 Place Color

Once the shapes of the letters have been perfected and the basic shapes of the cars drawn for accuracy, lightly begin placing color with a very sharp Verithin pencil. Beginning with Black, follow the illustration at right and try to apply the color as smoothly and evenly as possible.

For the blue around the 12 and the highlight in the rear gas cap, use True Blue, but switch to Indigo Blue for the Ford logo on the back.

Apply Prismacolor Canary Yellow to the strip on the rear of the car and into the yellow of the tires. Don't worry about the lettering on the tires at this stage. You'll be creating the lettering with Verithin Black in the next step.

Fill the tail light area with Pale Vermillion.

4 Deepen the Color

Continue deepening the tones of the car, filling in areas with Black. The Verithin Black will look a bit grainy at first, but will smooth out as you add more layers. Go into the tires next and create the lettering of Goodyear.

5 Finish the Drawing

To finish the drawing, deepen the tones until they fill in and the graininess is less noticeable. Study the finished art and the original photograph and locate the highlights. Don't fill these areas in. If you need to remove tone, use your kneaded eraser.

Use Crimson Red Verithin to create the decals on the front quarter panel next to the 12. These are very small and the wording is not easily seen, so create a representation of the words with patterns of light and dark instead.

The back window area is also a group of light and dark patterns. Use the True Blue and Black Verithins with a light touch and a sharp point. Don't forget to include the window straps.

For creative impact, try using a "border box" to finish the drawing. Place a box around the car, but allow the front and back bumpers to protrude beyond the line to create the illusion of depth. The Indigo Blue, True Blue and Violet in the corners act as a natural framework, leading the eye to the center of the picture and the car.

The shadow under the car is also important for creating depth and realism. Be sure to color in these tones smoothly and evenly, allowing them to become lighter as they move away from the car.

RYAN NEWMAN

2002 Raybestos Rookie of the Year

Ryan Newman drives for Penske Racing. In 2001, he competed in three divisions: ARCA, NASCAR Busch Series and NASCAR Winston Cup. In 2002, he entered the NASCAR Winston Cup Series full time and won the Raybestos Rookie of the Year title.

14"×17" (36cm × 43cm)
Graphite on 2-ply

#48—Jimmie Johnson

The #48 Lowes Chevrolet of Jimmie Johnson provides a great lesson on lettering (and an excellent example of how graphing your reference photo can help with accuracy). Because the letters are white, I chose to draw the car on white mat board. (Note: Prismacolor pencils are used except at the end of step 5.)

By looking at this car, you can see perspective at work again. Because it is a close-up shot taken straight on, the front of the car appears huge and the rear is hidden. Let the graph guide you as you draw.

Reference Photo

COLORS USED

Prismacolor. Light Cerulean Blue, Canary Yellow, Chartreuse, Crimson Red, Violet Blue, Indigo Blue, Black, True Blue, Cool Gray 50%, Orange, Aquamarine.

Verithin. Indigo Blue, Ultramarine, Black.

Other. No. 3 Nero pencil.

Graphed Reference Photo
To create brilliant color and shine, I like to use Prismacolors. This photo of the #48 Lowes Chevrolet is a perfect candidate for this technique. The bright shine on the front of the car and the deep, shiny colors of the rest of the vehicle lend themselves perfectly to the process of burnishing with Prismacolor.

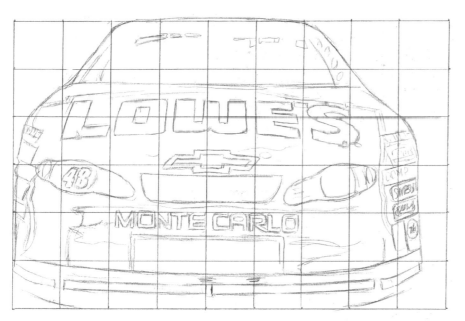

1 Use the Graph to Draw

Remember to draw not what you see but how you see it. Sketch the highlights across the windshield and the hood onto your drawing so you know where to keep color light later.

Gently remove the graph lines from the drawing using the kneaded eraser. Redraw any lines you may accidentally erase. When you're satisfied with the accuracy of your drawing, move on to the next step.

2 Secure Shapes

Always begin by outlining the lettering to make sure it is accurate. Clean up and correct the lines and angles around the word Lowes with a no. 3 Black Nero pencil. Start outlining some of the other dark areas to prepare them for the application of the other colors.

3 Begin Adding Color

Outline and fill the area around the word Monte Carlo with Light Cerulean Blue Prismacolor. Lighten the graphite lines to these letters first, double-checking their accuracy as you go. If you fill an area in with too much color, gently scrape off the excess with a very sharp craft knife.

Color the stripe on the bottom of the car Canary Yellow. The stripe curves as it reaches the side of the car and the color becomes a bit more green than yellow, so use Chartreuse for that area. Use the Chartreuse on the roof of the car where a hint of the number is showing. Add Canary Yellow to the 48 on the headlight decal and to the decals on the sides of the car.

Color the decals and the striping along the hood Crimson Red. With Violet Blue, start the deep color on the hood of the car and color the Chevy logo.

JIMMIE JOHNSON

Jimmie Johnson drives for the Hendrick Motorsports and Jeff Gordon, Inc. He made his first three Winston Cup starts in 2001. He went full time in the NASCAR Winston Cup Series in 2002. Johnson started thirty-one races and finished tenth in the point standings in six top-ten finishes.

16" × 20" (41cm × 51 cm)
Graphite on 4-ply board

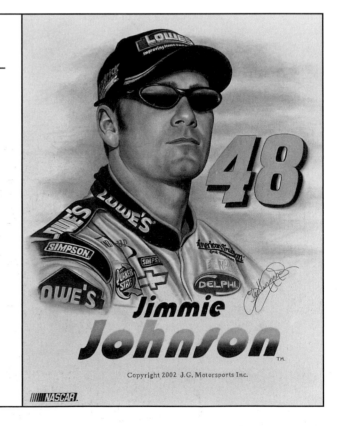

Copyright 2002 J.G. Motorsports Inc.

4 Deepen the Colors

The lighting in this picture is extreme: the top of the car is very dark while the front is shiny and bright. Because of the shadows, the dark blue of the car appears black along the windshield, so apply Black heavily there and also between the letters. Use Indigo Blue to transition from Black to Violet Blue.

Using the burnishing technique, continue filling in below the letters with the Violet Blue. Blend this color into the Indigo Blue and Black. Because the lighting changes, add a little True Blue to that area as well. Blend the True Blue into the Violet Blue to mix the colors together. Don't worry if this seems confusing—it doesn't have to be exact. Just study the reference photo to see the patterns created by the reflections of light. If yours aren't exactly the same, it shouldn't make a difference.

Add some Black to the windshield area, using Cool Gray 50% for the braces along the side of the window. Add Orange to the headlight decals.

5 Add Final Details

Finishing this picture is really just a process of filling in the blanks, much like a coloring book. Study the decals and do your best to represent their colors and letter placement, keeping in mind that the angle of the car is distorting the lettering.

For the grill areas, use Cool Gray 50% as a base color and then detail with Black.

For the shiny area in the bumper and on the air dam, add Aquamarine and burnish it into the True Blue and Blue Violet. Reflective areas created with multiple colors tend to look more authentic.

Once the car itself is complete, switch to Verithin pencils. Layer color all around the car to give the illusion of depth. Smoothly and evenly apply Indigo Blue, Ultramarine and Black to the background, letting the color fade as it moves farther from the car.

#18—Bobby Labonte

This car is a little more complicated than the others, particularly because of the lettering in the sponsor's name. The #18 Interstate Batteries Pontiac of Bobby Labonte has a lot of letters which makes accuracy even trickier. The grid method should help you size up the letters and place them correctly as you draw.

Perspective is obvious here, too. Take a look at the right side of the car. The lettering and numbers are unrecognizable due to the angle and the glare off the shiny surface. Artistically, I love this type of view because you can create an illusion with your pencils.

I created this drawing much the same way as the previous project. These colors, however, are less deep and intense. This car is in the bright sunlight and has a much lighter color scheme, so the drawing will appear differently when finished.

Don't worry if the drawing looks messy during the graphing stage. Once the lines are removed from the drawing paper, it will seem less cluttered and there's a lot of fine tuning done when applying colored pencil. (Note: Prismacolor pencils are used except where use of Verithin is indicated in step 5.)

COLORS USED

Prismacolor. Poppy Red, Pale Vermillion, Black, White, Apple Green, Grass Green, Cool Gray 50%, Cloud Blue.

Verithin. Black, Aquamarine, Indigo Blue, Grass Green.

Other. No. 3 Nero pencil.

Reference Photo

Graphed Reference Photo

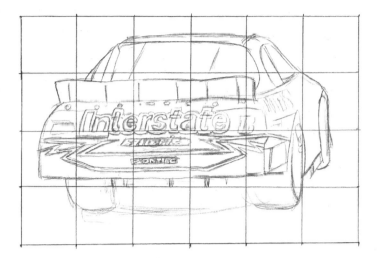

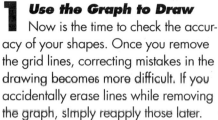
Use the Graph to Draw
Now is the time to check the accuracy of your shapes. Once you remove the grid lines, correcting mistakes in the drawing becomes more difficult. If you accidentally erase lines while removing the graph, simply reapply those later.

There is tiny lettering on this car. It is very difficult to outline small lettering at this stage. Some of the lettering will be easier to create while adding color.

Add the First Touches of Color
Start the drawing by filling in the lettering on the back of the car since everything else seems to connect them. Outline each letter with a no. 3 Nero pencil and compare with the reference photo for accuracy. Once you're satisfied with the results, fill in the letters, shading lightly enough to make corrections if needed. A typewriter eraser works well for cleaning up around the letters.

Move over to make the distorted letters on the right side of the car. The perspective makes them look awkward, which is how you need to draw them. It's difficult to draw things distorted from perspective like this, since you want to correct what your see, but keep the shapes as true to the photograph as you can. Also use the no. 3 Nero pencil to outline the wheel wells to establish the shape.

For the outer edge of the lettering and the number 18, use Poppy Red. Add Poppy Red accents to the roof and the side. The small round shapes on the back windows are holes for the track bar adjuster, which alters the pressure on the springs in the back of the car.

Apply Cloud Blue and Cool Gray 50% for the rear window. To capture the shine, add these colors with a heavy, burnished approach.

3 Add Panels of Color

Continue to add Poppy Red to the lower portion of the car. The area above it is a bit lighter in color, so use Pale Vermillion around the MBNA and the 18. The two colors are only a shade apart, but you can see the difference.

Use the no. 3 Nero pencil to color in the area around the *Pontiac*. When lettering is white, you'll find it easier to focus on the areas around the letters in order to create their shapes rather than outlining each letter individually.

4 Add Green

Continue with the rest of the paint scheme using two shades of green—the lighter Apple Green and the darker Grass Green. At this stage, adding color is much like filling in a coloring book. Use the Apple Green on the roof, sides and rear of the car. Color the fender Grass Green and add Grass Green accents to the roof, around the passenger side windows and a touch along the bumper and the rear edges of the car.

Color the metal under the car Cool Gray 70%, adding a streak along the back tire's rim, too.

With Black Prismacolor, continue blackening the area around the word Pontiac, moving on to shade the back tires.

For the passenger side windows, use Cloud Blue.

5 Finish by Detailing

Study the drawing closely to see how the details are cleaned up. Sharpen the edges so they're crisp and fill in colors. Apply White across the word Interstate to make this area look shiny. To recreate the glare of sunlight across the car's reflective surface, burnish the right side of the car with White, blurring the shapes.

Small details, like the lines around the MBNA and 18, are important. Use a straightedge to make them even and straight.

Simplify the drawing by leaving out the background from the photo. Instead, layer Verithin colors Black, Indigo Blue, Aquamarine and Grass Green around the car and bring out the green. A line for the horizon and a line for the road complete the drawing.

BOBBY LABONTE

Bobby Labonte's first career NASCAR Winston Cup victory came in 1995 in the Coca-Cola 600 at Charlotte, North Carolina. The #18 has won at least one race every year since. Labonte earned the title NASCAR Winston Cup champion in 2000.

16" × 20" (41cm × 51cm)
Prismacolor on suede mat board

#97—Kurt Busch

Now that we've explored drawing NASCAR vehicles at various angles, let's try one from the side where the whole car is visible. From this perspective, the advertising potential of a NASCAR vehicle becomes clear. This perspective also shows the streamlined body of the cars of today, a look totally different from the old boxy styles of years gone by.

But when I look over the photograph of Kurt Busch's #97 Sharpie Ford from an artist's point of view, other elements catch my eye. For example, the strong sunlight casts an incredible shadow beneath the car. For an artist, a shadow is a gift that will make the artwork look awesome!

Reference Photo

Graphed Reference Photo

COLORS USED

Prismacolor. Crimson Red, Poppy Red, Canary Yellow, Sunburst Yellow, True Blue, White, Black, Cool Gray 50%.

Verithin. True Blue, Grass Green, True Green, Indigo Blue, Orange, Black.

Other. No. 3 Nero pencil.

1 Check for Accuracy and Remove Graph

This view shows all the decals on the car, something nearly impossible to depict accurately with freehand illustration, especially at this scale. Focus on the larger ones. The tinier ones can be less detailed, as long as they have the shape and color represented.

Because the tires appear as perfect circles from this perspective, use a template to create their edges.

Carefully remove the grid lines from your drawing and redraw any shapes that you may accidentally erase.

DRIVER'S WINDOW

When drawing cars from the side, the driver's window will be in view. Rather than a window made of glass, a nylon mesh net is installed in the window opening. This can be a challenge to draw. Up close, you can see the weave, but from a distance, the weave is not so obvious.

2 Start Filling in Color

Begin by carefully outlining all of the letters and window areas with a sharpened no. 3 Nero pencil. Outline the 97 with a sharp Crimson Red Prismacolor pencil. Use the same color for the tip of the Sharpie marker on the rear quarter panel.

When drawing a dark colored car, start with the lightest colors first. Use your Prismacolor Canary Yellow and Sunburst Yellow to fill in the areas with yellow lettering. Don't worry about the shapes of the yellow letters too much; you'll create

them later with a black pencil.

Color the red decals between the 97 and the front tire with the lighter Poppy Red Verithin pencil. For the blue stripe, use True Blue.

3 Color the Decals

Since the decals on this car are so small, add them with the tip of sharp Verithin pencils. The point of a Prismacolor pencil is simply too thick for this type of detail. Once the decals are created, fill in the rest of the car with Black Prismacolor. White works well for the shiny areas inside the rear window and the front window vent.

Continue adding details to the car. Add blue areas to the roof, trunk area and hood with True Blue. These shapes are small and illegible, but their placement is very important.

For the smaller details and decals, use Verithin pencils. For example, use Grass Green Verithin for the "W" in the WM decal and Orange Verithin on the head-

light and tail light. Add a shadow under the car using Black Verithin to give the drawing a feel of realism.

Start to create the window netting with Cool Gray 50% Prismacolor. You'll finish this up in the next step with Black.

Use a graphite pencil to sketch in lines for the background.

4 *Add Final Details*

To finish this piece, use a combination of Verithin and Prismacolor pencils.

Before you begin the background, continue adding small details to the car and filling in the color for a smooth look. Except for the areas on the window already colored white, leave paper exposed in all the white areas rather than filling in with a pencil. This is less likely to smear and once the other colors are applied, it'll be easy to clean up with a typewriter eraser.

The converging lines of the background create the illusion of speed and movement. Use a straightedge and some imagination to give this artwork some flare. Once again, layer the background colors smoothly with the sharp points of the Verithin pencils.

KURT BUSCH

Kurt Busch made his NASCAR Winston Cup debut in 2000. He came to the forefront of NASCAR Winston Cup racing with 20 top-10 finishes in 36 starts. He finished the year fourth in the NASCAR Winston Cup standings, trailing series champion Tony Stewart by only 159 points. Kurt drives for Roush Racing.

14" × 17" (36cm × 43cm)
Graphite on 4-ply bristol

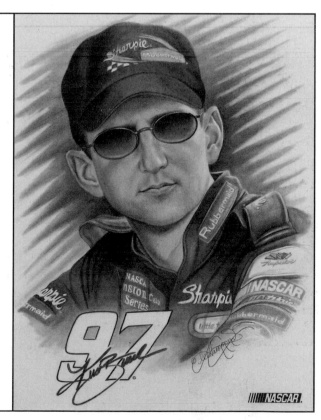

#24—Jeff Gordon

Jeff Gordon's #24 DuPont Chevrolet is fun to draw because of its bright colors. One of the biggest challenges is curbing the creativity that all that color provokes! I chose to use no. 971 Daffodil mat board for this project. The bright-colored background will help make the vivid colors jump out.

The angle of the car is interesting, too. Notice how the car recedes and appears smaller toward the back.

COLORS USED

Prismacolor. Yellow Chartreuse, Canary Yellow, Poppy Red, True Blue, Copenhagen Blue, White, Black, Cool Gray 50%, Orange, Yellow Ochre.

Verithin. Grass Green, Orange, Sunburst Yellow, Poppy Red, Carmine Red, Black, True Blue, Canary Yellow.

Reference Photo

Graphed Reference Photo

1 Use the Graph to Draw

You have to start with the line drawing as a foundation; you can't skip straight to the colors. Use the graph to produce an accurate line drawing. Pay attention to the perspective and the way the numbers and letters appear on the side of the car.

Once the line drawing is accurate, gently remove the graph lines with a kneaded eraser. Repair any lines that may have been accidentally erased in the process.

2 Add Lightest Colors First

Start drawing with the lightest colors first. For the 24 on the side of the car, the smaller 24 on the headlight and for the area on the roof, use Yellow Chartreuse. Look closely at the flames and you'll see that the very edges are yellow. Color this area, some of the decals and the lettering on the tires Canary Yellow. Color the other decals—including the DuPont, Ford and Monte Carlo logos— White.

Once these lighter colors are in place, begin edging the headlights and logos on the front of the car with Poppy Red.

3 Fill in Color

Continue with the Poppy Red, burnishing in the color. In the shiny areas, like the curved portion around the passenger side headlight, apply White firmly to create a reflection and the illusion of an edge.

With True Blue, apply color around the flames and shade both the windshield and the headlight. The blue inside the DuPont logo is a little darker, so use Copenhagen Blue to fill this area. Keep the edges of your lettering crisp and clean. Detail the side panel with a little Copenhagen Blue.

Study the reference photo to see where the colors might be affected by highlights or shadows. Using White, burnish the highlighted areas in the windshield, along the side of the car and in the front end.

VICTORY LANE

To make your artwork really stand out, add enhancements like the checkered floor from Victory Lane.

4 Complete the Car

To make the windshield look more reflective, burnish the area with some Aquamarine and White Prismacolor. Also use some Cool Gray 50% to maintain the illusion of window netting and the internal structure of the car. Define the window straps with Black and White. Use the same colors—Aquamarine, Cool Gray 50%, White—in the headlight decals.

To make the side of the car look realistic, use a darker blue than you did on the hood to make it look shadowed. Copenhagen Blue works well for this. Use True Blue toward the back of the car where light is reflecting.

For the small details of the decals, use Verithin pencils in Grass Green, Orange, Sunburst Yellow, Poppy Red, Carmine Red and Black. To make the decals look like they're in the distance, burnish them with White Prismacolor.

To create the fine line along the hood, use a sharp craft knife to gently etch the edge. This gives you a finer line than you could possibly draw.

The background halo of color really makes the car stand out. Lightly layer using Verithin pencils. Use True Blue and Black Verithin under the car, switching to Grass Green towards the top and the back. Gently fade into Canary Yellow to blend the halo with the yellow hue of the paper.

#3—Dale Earnhardt

The #3 Chevrolet driven by Dale Earnhardt might just be the most popular car in racing history. At my first race in Texas, I had the pleasure of watching the "Intimidator" race this car. None of the photos I took

that day were large enough for this lesson, so I drew from another reference. Instead of using a graphed photo, I've provided a graphed reference of my finished artwork.

1 Draw All the Elements

Draw the car as precisely as possibly. All the decals should be spaced properly in proportion to each other and the lettering drawn as you see it, not as you know it. Notice the 3 on the rear of the car, how odd it looks because of the perspective. Lightly sketch in any shadows and highlights you see, just enough to indicate where you'll darken or burnish the colors later.

Once the drawing is consistent with the car, erase all the grid lines with a kneaded eraser. If any lines are accidentally erased in the process, draw them back in freehand.

2 Add the First Layer of Color

Begin your drawing by detailing the lettering for accuracy. With a very sharp no. 3 Nero pencil, rework the shapes of the Goodwrench logo (note how the gas cap interferes with the H) as well as all the smaller lettering. Use a sharp Crimson Red Prismacolor for the red areas, like the 3 on the door and the lettering on the hood. For the window and the gray stripe along the lower edge of the car, use Prismacolor Cool Gray 50%.

If you look at the reference drawing, you will see that even though the car is black, color is clearly reflected along the top edges. Use Aquamarine Prismacolor for these reflections. Also use Aquamarine in the headlight and the small logo toward the rear of the car.

For the Burger King logo, use Sunburst Yellow and Crimson Red. Color the Food City logo with Ultramarine Blue. Fill the Good Year lettering with Canary Yellow and remember to edge these small letters with Black later.

3 Fill in Color

Start to fill in the car with Black Prismacolor, going around small details with a very sharp point. This stage can be tedious, but take your time and draw for accuracy. For the tiny decals, use Verithin pencils with very sharp points. For any of the white areas, leave the paper exposed so you can simply clean up with a typewriter eraser when you are finished.

The small details of a race car are an accumulation of very small shapes much like a puzzle. Although it can be somewhat confusing and tedious, it is important to include all the small shapes and colors. Starting with the top of the car, use Warm Gray 50% for the distorted 3 and outline in Crimson Red. Use Warm Gray 50% on the trunk and hood of the car, too.

Outline the edges of the car and crisp up the shapes with Black. Start outlining the lettering and filling in the Black to deepen the tone of the car. Include some Aquamarine along with the Black to make the car appear reflective. Also use the Black in the window area to start developing the window netting as well as the decals next to the windows. Place the shadow under the car to help define the bottom edge of the car. Use Cool Gray 50% to place the second stripe along the lower edge.

Use Yellow Ochre in the tail light and on the tires. These tires are in motion, so the lettering of Goodyear is blurred. On a motionless car, the letters would show and even appear to be a brighter color, like Canary Yellow. Motion "grays" the color and all detail is lost.

To make the wheels look reflective, add some Orange and Aquamarine. This use of reflective, repetitive colors is what makes your artwork look convincing.

To finish the decals, use Verithin pencils in Poppy Red, Carmine Red, Canary Yellow and Ultramarine Blue. Color the AV below the Snap-On logo with Poppy Red.

Start filling in the roundness of the tires with Black Verithin.

4 Add the Finishing Touches

To finish the piece realistically, burnish the Black to make it look shiny. Because Black makes everything else stand out, it is very important to study the decals carefully before drawing them and clean them up for accuracy. Fill in and burnish the tires and apply Crimson Red and Aquamarine to the rims. Don't forget the small color areas, like the Grass Green in the Gatorade decal.

Burnish the headlights with White over the Aquamarine and Poppy Red. Continue using White to burnish in a shiny impression in the rear bumper, rear spoiler, rear window, hood, trunk and top. Aquamarine is a common color to use as a reflection in Black. Study the car to find all the places to use it, like along the edge of the window and inside the gas cap area.

You'll notice a lot of Aquamarine. To create the ridge through the 3 on the door, draw a line with Light Gray Verithin through the number using a straightedge to keep it nice and even.

To really make this car stand out, create a border box and repeat some of the colors from the car into the background. Use a straightedge to create the ground definition. With very sharp Verithin pencils (I used Indigo Blue, Ultramarine Blue, Black and Crimson Red), layer color below the car. Above and behind the car, use Poppy Red and Crimson Red. The result is a bright box of color that leads the eye right into the car!

DALE EARNHARDT

Dale Earnhardt was a dynamic driver known as the "Intimidator," a title he earned for his intense dedication to winning. With 76 career victories and 7 NASCAR Winston Cup Championships to his credit, Earnhardt is truly a legend. In February 2001, Earnhardt died in a crash at the Daytona 500. He will be forever remembered and missed in the stock car world.

14"×17" (36cm × 43cm)
Graphite on 2-ply bristol

Chapter Five

PIT ROAD

Behind the Scenes

I want to take this opportunity to tell you some of the "facts." For those of you who already have a good understanding of NASCAR racing, this may seem like going back to kindergarten. However, for those new to the sport, these facts may be interesting.

One of the most exciting aspects of the race is the action in pit road. I have been fortunate enough to be allowed access to the pit area and to work alongside the pit crews. I want to thank my friend Darryl Lomick, one of the NASCAR Officials, for allowing me this opportunity. It provided me with many interesting shots.

When pulling into pit road in the middle of a race, the driver must be able to identify his "stall" immediately. He has been racing at speeds of over 150 miles per hour and must slow to 65 to 45 mph to enter pit road (depending on the track). The driver looks for his "pit board" extended over his pit stall. When looking at the pit boards, you may wonder why they are full of holes! This keeps them from flapping in the wind.

A driver can "pit" any time his car is experiencing trouble. This robs the driver of valuable time and sends him further back in the field. A driver can become "lapped" by the faster cars, and this time is hard to make up.

The drivers can also pit anytime there is a caution flag on the track, taking advantage of another driver's misfortune. If all is going smoothly, the entire field will pit under a green flag pit stop, allowing everyone to refuel and replace tires.

Pulling in for Service
As the driver comes on to pit road, he must know where to pull in for service. Each driver must look for the flag that identifies his stall.

Movement of Flags
The holes in the pit stop flag keep it steady in the wind. You can see the difference when comparing it to the American flag next to it.

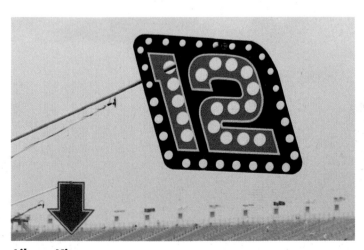

Like a Kite
Without the holes, the stiff material the flags are made of would take off like a kite.

Our Pit Road Tour Guide
Lee Hammond with NASCAR Official, Darryl Lomick.

The Pit Crew

When drawing the "inside," fast-paced action of NASCAR, it is important to show a lot of "movement." This is done by analyzing the way things are moving, and what elements are coming together to create the look of action. When drawing this pit stop scene, I took note of two important things. The first one was the positioning of the crew. Look at the motion of their bodies as they rush toward the car. Look at the tilt of the tire handler as he moves into position. Also, the wrench being thrown in mid-air behind him adds to the overall look of motion.

I also took note of the shadows underneath the men and the car. They give the illusion of bright sunlight above them, and repeat the active shapes of the crew.

I wanted the pit crew to stand out in this drawing, so I minimized the background and made their colors very vibrant (not hard to do with bright red uniforms!).

When drawing things that are far in the distance, the details are less distinct. When viewing the crowds in the stands, you can see how the people have been reduced to blurs of color and patterns. I used Verithin pencils for everything in the background to give it less detail and a grainy effect, allowing the bright colors of the pit crew to remain the main focus of the drawing. While drawing, I analyzed the look of the crowd scenes. I found that the prevalent colors are usually red, white, blue and gray.

The pit crew is essential to winning races. Each member has a specific role to play, and it must be carried out with flawless perfection. The crew is like a choreographed dance team, and they practice over and over so their maneuvers are executed smoothly and quickly. Each pit stop is only between ten and twenty seconds long. And a lot of work is done in those few seconds.

Seven crew members are allowed over the wall at one time. The wall is two feet high. If anyone jumps over the wall before the car has come to a complete stop, they will be issued a penalty. Each pit stall has a NASCAR Official who monitors all movement and procedures.

The following illustrations will show you what each crew member does.

The Illusion of Movement

The illusion of movement is what makes a drawing interesting. The fast-paced motion of this pit crew is captured here.

The background colors are made dull, to make them recede. To capture the crowd scene, I used the side of my pencil to blur the look.

The "Action!"

8" x 10" (20cm x 25cm)
Prismacolor and Verithin pencils on no. 3297 Arctic White mat board

COLORS USED

Prismacolor. Poppy Red, Crimson Red, Black, White, Mediterranean Blue.

Verithin. Black, Indigo Blue, Grass Green, Carmine Red.

Members of the Team

The driver is not completely alone in his vehicle. His radio keeps him in close contact with his crew chief, and his "spotters." Spotters are members of the race crew that are strategically placed high above the speedway on a tower or in a press box. They tell the driver everything about the "traffic" and track conditions that the driver is unable to physically see from his car.

The crew chief monitors the race and the driver, and is in constant radio contact with his crew, the driver and the NASCAR Officials.

Each pit stall is equipped with high-tech computer equipment that analyzes almost every aspect of the car.

The Spotter
The spotters are crucial to the driver and act as their extended "eyes."

An Official and a Fireman
In every pit stall, you will see a NASCAR Official as well as a fireman. Both are necessary to monitor and handle everything in the pit stop, which can be a dangerous area.

The Crew Chief
The crew chief is the mastermind of the entire team. He coordinates and manages all aspects of the team, crew, car and driver. He sits on top of the big tool box located in the pit stall.

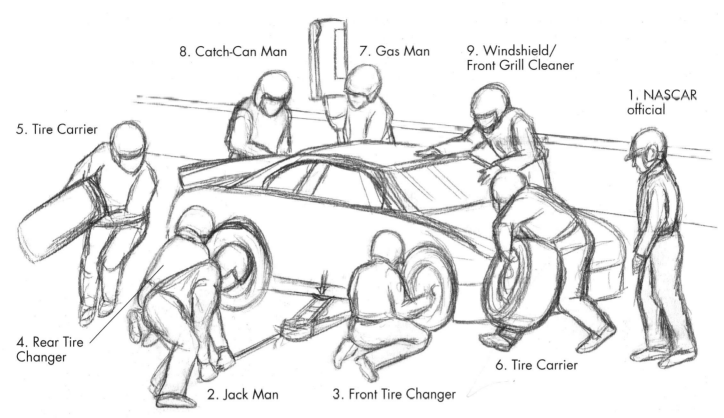

8. Catch-Can Man   **7. Gas Man**   **9. Windshield/ Front Grill Cleaner**

1. NASCAR official

5. Tire Carrier

4. Rear Tire Changer

6. Tire Carrier

2. Jack Man   **3. Front Tire Changer**

Team Members

Bringing in a victory takes many talented people. Each member of the pit crew carries out his duties with precision and speed.

1. NASCAR Official. He monitors all stall activity, ready to issue penalties if rules are not followed to the letter!

2. Jack Man. The jack man hoists the right side of the car first for the tire changers. Look for the small arrow on all cars—this is where he inserts the jack. When the right-side tires are changed, he rushes to the driver's side to do the same thing.

3. Front Tire Changer. With an air wrench, the front tire changer removes the lug nuts from the right side tire first, removes the tire, replaces it with a fresh one, and then replaces the lug nuts. He then races to the driver's side to do the same.

4. Rear Tire Changer. The rear tire changer follows the same procedure as the

front tire changer. When the tires have been changed, both tire changers raise one arm to signal that they are finished.

5 & 6. The Tire Carriers. The front and back tire carriers carry fresh tires to the right side of the car. They then carry the used tires to the wall, and deposit them, picking up fresh ones for the driver's side.

7 & 8. The Gas Man and Catch-Can Man. These men work together to refuel the car. The gas can man carries a large gas can (11 gallons/42 liters) and inserts the nozzle into the gas tank. The catch-can man inserts an overflow container to prevent spilling onto pit road. The catch-can man takes over as the gas man returns to the wall for a second can of gas. When the first can is empty, the catch-can man removes it, and returns the empty can to the wall. The gas man dumps the second can and, when it is empty, removes the can and overflow container. He raises his arm

when he is finished as a signal to the official and the jack man.

9. Windshield/Front Grill Cleaner. Sometimes the windshield or front grill needs to be cleaned. An eighth crew member is allowed to do this, but only with an official's permission.

When all duties have been performed by each crew member, and each has an arm raised, the jack man will lower the driver's side of the car. As soon as the car hits the pavement, the driver is free to go. All crew members give the car a push in case of stalling. When the car has left, all debris is cleaned up and swept away, and all tools returned behind the wall. Then the crew members patiently wait for the next stop.

NASCAR Helmets

In every pit stall you will see a NASCAR Official as well as a fireman. Both are necessary to monitor and handle every aspect of a pit stop, which is an extremely dangerous situation. Everyone, including all crew members, must wear protective, fire-retardant uniforms and helmets.

As an artist, I found this helmet of particular interest. The colors reflecting in the face shield are spectacular, and provide a wonderful exercise for using Prismacolor pencils. I loved burnishing all these colors together to create this drawing. Have fun as you draw this helmet step by step.

Reference Photo

COLORS USED

Prismacolor. Canary Yellow, Poppy Red, Crimson Red, Pale Vermillion, Mahogany Red, Yellow Ochre, Process Red, Aquamarine, White, Ultramarine Blue, Imperial Violet, Black.

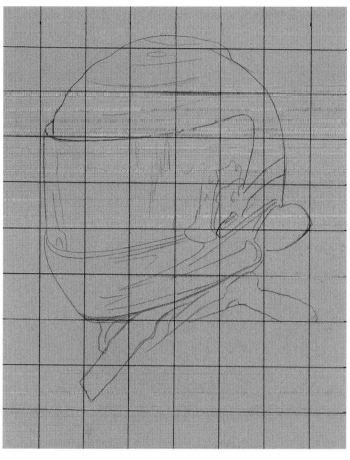

1 Graph and Draw the Helmet

Using the same graphing procedure from the previous projects, create an accurate line drawing of this helmet. This is more an experiment with color blending, so feel free to leave off the manufacturer stickers and lettering.

2 Add Color

Once you have drawn the outline and removed the graph, apply the lighter colors of the helmet, starting with Canary Yellow and Poppy Red.

Continue burnishing with heavy pressure to fill in the Poppy Red. Add the darker red ridges of the helmet with Crimson Red. For the lighter areas between the ridges, use Pale Vermillion.

In the chin area of the helmet, use Mahogany Red and Pale Vermillion with Yellow Ochre to add shadow to the bright yellow.

Apply color to the face mask with Pale Vermillion, Process Red and Aquamarine.

3 Add More Color

With Pale Vermillion, Process Red and Aquamarine, start to apply color to the face mask. Add Pale Vermillion and Crimson Red to create the look of ridges along the top. Work on the chin area of the helmet and begin placing colors in the face mask.

4 Burnish the Colors

Continue adding color and burnish them together.

Can you see how in the upper portion of the helmet I have continued adding Crimson Red to make it richer in hue? Always use a lighter color to burnish the darker ones in. In this case, blend in the Crimson Red with both Poppy Red and Pale Vermillion. For the very bright highlights, add some White.

Continue adding brilliant color to the face mask, working in more Aquamarine, some Ultramarine Blue and some Imperial Violet.

5 Finish the Drawing

To finish this drawing, keep adding color, both dark and light, until you feel satisfied. Burnish the colors into your work, using light over dark. Do not add Black until all colors are completed.

When you are finished, you will have a wonderfully brilliant and reflective piece of artwork!

Chapter Six

AROUND THE TRACK

MIDWEST THUNDERFEST 2002

PRICE CHOPPER

TAURUS

KANSAS CITY

The Pace Car

NASCAR race cars are not the only vehicles at the track sporting a vibrant paint scheme. This is a drawing of the Official Pace Car used at the inaugural race of the Kansas Speedway in September of 2001. The beautiful blue color, along with the American flag, made for a striking pace car and tribute to 9/11 (this was the first race after the tragedies.)

I used Prismacolor to burnish in the bright, vibrant colors, and a lavender paper to make the white areas stand out more. Using dark colors behind the car makes the highlight areas appear brighter, and creates the illusion of bright sunlight. To make the image even more realistic, I placed the reflection of the sky and clouds into the windows of the car.

Whenever you are drawing cars, remember that they have very shiny surfaces. Reflections are everything!

The Official Pace Car
This was the Official Pace Car for the Protection 400 race at the Kansas Speedway, the inaugural race in 2001. This car was used as a tribute to the tragedies of 9/11.

Follow the Pace Car

The pace car is an important part of the race. It leads the cars around the track at the beginning of the race at a consistent speed. Acceleration can only occur and racing can only begin after the pace car has entered pit road. Until then, speeds must stay consistent.

The pace car also comes out during cautions to keep the cars together and lined up until the track is safe again. Once the pace car returns to pit road, racing resumes.

Official Pace Car
This was the pace car for the last race of 2002 in Homestead, Florida.

Not Quite a Rolling Billboard, But ...
Even though the pace car can't compete with the race cars in advertising capability, there is some lettering on the door that can provide some graphing practice.

98

On the Pole

Before each race, there is a day for practice and for qualifying. In practice, the teams get the cars ready to race, making adjustments to their engines and checking overall vehicle performance. In qualifying, the cars run one at a time and their speed is clocked. The car with the fastest time will take the best starting position for the upcoming race.

There is a term in racing called "being on the pole." The pole is the vertical scoring mechanism that displays the track positions as the drivers are racing. Being "on the pole" during qualifying refers to the driver who qualified for the race with the highest speed. His score is placed at the top of the pole. He then has the best starting position, which is in front on the outside.

On the Pole
The race hasn't started so there's no one "on the pole" in this picture. The painted numbers indicate position—first place, second place, etc.—and the digital numbers indicate which car is in that position. The numbers are adjust every time the cars cross the start/finish line as they circle the track.

"Banking" and "Drafting"

When cars run close together, you will hear the term "drafting." This is when the cars in the front block the wind from the cars behind them. Without the wind resistance, the cars trailing behind have an easier time—and actually conserve fuel. Being in second can be good sometimes for these reasons.

While watching a NASCAR race, you might also hear the term "banking." This refers to the slope of the racetrack. Tracks slope inward toward the infield, which helps the drivers control their cars around the curves. This slope varies in degree from track to track, and is much more extreme than you may think. When walking on the track, sometimes it is so steep, it is difficult to walk without falling down.

Drafting
The cars line up behind the leader, letting the first car do all the work.

Banking
9" × 12" (23cm × 30cm)
Prismacolor and Verithin
pencils on no. 3310
Regent Gray mat board

Flags Flown at the Track

These are two of my favorite flags! With NASCAR becoming America's favorite sport, both of these flags are symbolic of NASCAR.

The rolling fabric of flags makes it a good subject for artists. The way the fabric moves changes the patterns dramatically. You can see how the stars and stripes of the American flag change with the creases and folds. It is important to study these patterns when drawing, following them in and out of the fabric.

The same movement can be seen with the checkerboard. You can see the curve of the folds in the shapes of the black and white squares.

Both of these drawings were done with Prismacolor to make them look vivid, but I used Verithin in the background to create the illusion of sky.

COLORS USED

Prismacolor. Poppy Red, Crimson Red, Indigo Blue, Cool Gray 50%, White, Black.

Verithin. True Blue.

The American Flag and The Checkered Flag
16" × 10" (41cm × 25cm)
Prismacolor pencils on no. 3297 Arctic White mat board

The Flag Man

Flag Man

There are other flags in NASCAR that are very important. The race is monitored by the NASCAR Officials, and the flag man notifies the drivers of the racing conditions through the use of various colored flags. The flag man is positioned over the start/finish line of the track. Each flag he displays represents a different track condition.

The Flag Man

11" x 14" (28cm x 36cm)
Prismacolor pencils on Coal Black Artagain drawing paper

The Language of Flags

THE GREEN FLAG

The flag man coordinates with the pace car. At the beginning of the race, the cars have to maintain their position in the field by following the pace car. They can race as soon as the pace car leaves the track and enters pit road. The flag man then waves the green flag to tell the drivers to accelerate as they cross the start/finish line. Let the racing begin!

THE YELLOW FLAG

The yellow flag is displayed immediately when a caution is declared. It is important to race to the flag when it is displayed, because as soon as you cross the start/finish line, the pace car keeps you in single file position until the race starts again. Where you end up in line is where you will restart.

Following the Pace Car
The Official Pace Car leads the cars around the track at the Kansas Speedway.

Green Flag
Let the racing begin!

Yellow Flag
Caution on the racetrack. Get behind the pace car!

WHITE FLAG

The white flag indicates that the race leader has crossed the start/finish line to begin the last lap of the race. If the white and yellow flag are shown at the same time, it means the race will end under caution.

RED FLAG

If the conditions are such that it is completely unsafe to race, the red flag will be displayed. All cars must come to a stop behind the pace car, and no work on the car is allowed.

BLACK FLAG

This is the flag no driver wants to see. It indicates that a certain car must return to the pit or garage. It can also indicate that a driver's actions will not be tolerated. If a driver ignores this flag (a huge no-no!), another black flag with a white cross is displayed, taking away points for that driver. Fortunately, this flag is seldom seen.

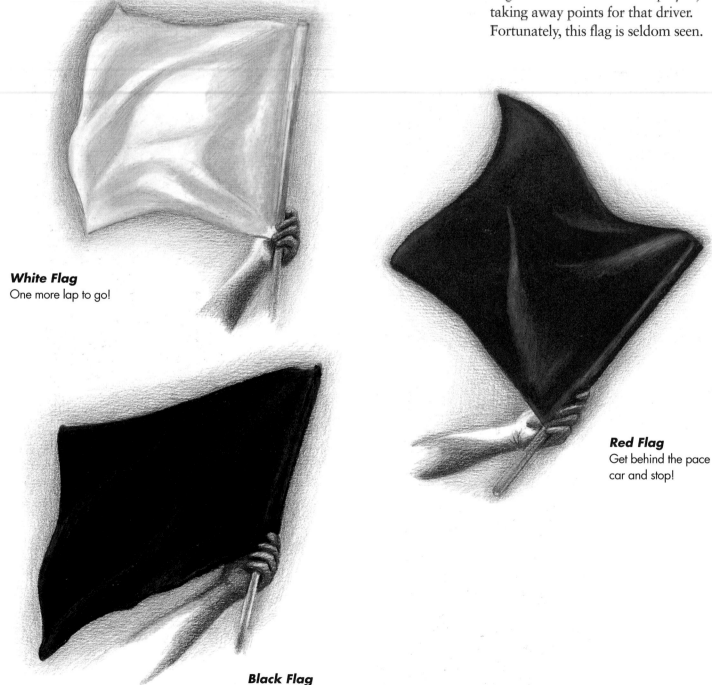

White Flag
One more lap to go!

Red Flag
Get behind the pace car and stop!

Black Flag
Head in to Pit Road!

PASSING FLAG

This is a passing flag. In most races, you have some cars that are not as fast as the others. When faster vehicles are trying to overtake "lapped" vehicles, the flag man will show this flag to let the slower drivers know to pull over and allow the race leaders to pass.

CHECKERED FLAG

This is the universal symbol for racing of all kinds. Whenever you see checkered flags—either alone or in pairs—some kind of race is taking place. It is the ultimate symbol of man's need to compete and win.

The checkered flag is waved only when the first place car crosses the finish line, signaling a win and the end of the race.

RACING ATTITUDE

When races take place, everyone and everything takes on a racing attitude. At a recent race I attended, I noticed that even the trash cans were a reminder of the big event!

Passing Flag
Move over and allow faster cars to pass.

Seeing Checkered Flags Everywhere
First one to the trash can wins!

Checkered Flag
Every driver's favorite flag!

Speed

When someone says the word "NASCAR" to me, the first thing that comes to my mind is SPEED! I had no idea what speed really was until I went to my first NASCAR race. Watching the race on TV is very exciting, but it doesn't do the speed justice. It is something you actually "feel" as the cars go by!

A funny situation put the essence of speed into perspective for me. I was doing a promotion and charity auction with Jeff Gordon, who needed to return to the racetrack once all the autographs had been signed. The track was a good thirty-five miles away, but he chose to drive his own car rather than take a traditional helicopter. For the sake of security, a police motorcade escorted us. I rode in the lead police car, chatting with the officer as we sped down the highway. Eventually, the officer (who didn't realize we were escorting a NASCAR driver) pointed out how fast we were going, saying he hoped that the celebrity back there didn't think the local police were speed demons.

At that moment, it dawned on me: Jeff drove three times that speed for four solid hours at a time! I laughed and told the officer not to worry; a guy like Jeff Gordon probably wouldn't notice we were exceeding the speed limit by about five miles per hour.

To produce the essence of speed in your artwork, you have to understand what makes things look like they are moving. Our eyes can only focus on one "level" or "plane" at a time. Focusing on a moving object like a race car will blur the background of the crowd in the grandstands. Focusing on the crowd will blur the car.

I recommend using that blurring effect to make the car look like it's speeding. Study this drawing of Dale Earnhardt's #3 GM Goodwrench Chevrolet as it zooms across the paper. I used the method of streaking to give it the illusion of movement.

After completing the car, I crossed horizontal lines of White and True Blue Prismacolor right over the car. And as if the penciled streaks weren't enough, I also scraped away color with a craft knife to create a few more. Take great care when using this technique. It takes practice to do it without gouging the paper. And it takes courage to scrape a pretty drawing!

Dale Earnhardt's #3
Using dark colors in the background gives the drawing an ominous look, which is very fitting for the #3 car of the "Intimidator"!

Dale Earnhardt's #3 GM Goodwrench Chevrolet
16"×20" (41cm × 51cm)
Prismacolor pencil on no. 3297 Arctic White mat board

COLORS USED

Prismacolor. White, Black, True Blue, Indigo Blue, Ultramarine Blue, Crimson Red, Poppy Red, Canary Yellow, Orange, Cool Gray 50%, Sunburst Yellow.

Streaks of Speed

Indicate Banking

I used streaking in this illustration also, but it is kept in the background.

The curved streaks of color represent the banking of the racetrack and give the illusion of the curve of the racetrack. To create these streaks in the background, layer the Verithin pencil colors one over another and then "draw" the color out with a typewriter eraser.

The overlapping of the vehicles also gives dimension and perspective to the artwork. Burnish the cars in the back with White to make them look blurred and less detailed. They are also much smaller in size.

Drafting Around the Turn
16" x 20" (41cm x 51cm)
Prismacolor and Verithin pencils on no.1008 Ivory mat board

> **COLORS USED**
>
> *Prismacolor.* Ultramarine Blue, Indigo Blue, True Blue, White, Black, Crimson Red, Carmine Red, Poppy Red, Canary Yellow.
>
> *Verithin.* Indigo Blue, Black, Carmine Red, Scarlet Red, Dahlia Purple.

Indicate Speed With the Background

Streaks of Color

In this example, I used the crowd in the background to create the illusion of speed for me. First, I streaked Prismacolor pencils horizontally to create bright blobs of color and then I burnished heavily with White, giving the illusion that the cars are zooming by. To create a look of acceleration, I also added some white streaks behind the #97 Sharpie car.

In this scene, the #6 Viagra car driven by Mark Martin and the #97 Sharpie car driven by Kurt Busch race for the lead side by side. The blue, black and white color scheme on each car emphasizes the fact that they both race for the Roush team.

Roush Teammates Take the Lead!
Mark Martin (#6) and Kurt Busch (#97)
12" × 16" (31cm × 41cm)
Prismacolor pencils on no. 3297 Arctic White mat board

COLORS USED

Prismacolor. (Crowd) Crimson Red, Pale Vermillion, Sunburst Yellow, Orange, Canary Yellow, True Blue, Periwinkle, Black, White.

(Cars) Carmine Red, Periwinkle, Imperial Violet, Crimson Red, Canary Yellow, Orange, Black, White.

(Wall and Track) Warm Gray 50%, Cool Gray 70%, Slate Blue, Black, White.

Extreme Speed

Speed in Black and White

To create extreme speed, all the details must be sacrificed. Even in black and white, this is an intriguing depiction of NASCAR racing. None of the recognizable details of individual drivers remain, only the feel of the race.

SPEED

8" × 16" (20cm × 41cm)
Prismacolor on no. 3297 Arctic White mat board

COLORS USED

Prismacolor. Black, White.

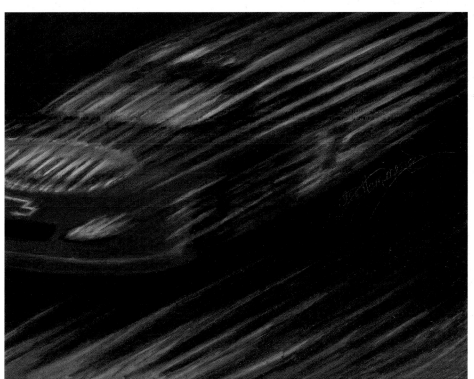

Speed in Color

The extreme blur is also possible in color. Even though the details have been obliterated, the viewer still knows that this is the #24 DuPont car of Jeff Gordon. The black background intensifies the drawing. It's almost as if the car has been shot out of a cannon into the night!

Gordon

8" × 10" (20cm × 25cm)
Prismacolor pencils on Gray illustration board

COLORS USED

Prismacolor. Crimson Red, Poppy Red, Pale Vermillion, Cool Gray 20%, Canary Yellow, Mediterranean Blue, True Blue, Black, White.

Other Speed Elements

Sudden Speed

Sometimes only part of the car needs to be blurred. In this rendering, the Sharpie emblem is clearly visible, as well as the other decals, but the speed is depicted in the rear. The streaks coming off the tire and back of the car give the illusion of the car moving away, just as if taking off from a pit stop.

Peeling Out!

8" x 16" (20cm x 41cm)
Prismacolor on no. 3297 Arctic White mat board

COLOR USED

Prismacolor. Crimson Red, Carmine Red, Poppy Red, True Blue, Indigo Blue, Canary Yellow, Cool Gray 50%, Cool Gray 70%, Black, White.

Motionless Elements

The illusion of speed can still be created even when including elements that aren't moving, or aren't even real. This drawing of Dale Jarrett's #88 UPS Ford combined with the checkered flag is a good example. The gentle wave of the flag, in addition to the streaks coming off of his car, makes a neat presentation. To make it even more interesting, and fitting to his corporate sponsor, I used brown tones to create this drawing. UPS uses the color brown as a marketing tool. Because of this, I chose to make the checkered flag brown and white instead of black and white.

The black streaks contrast with the brown tones for impact. The contrast keeps the streaks from getting lost in the background. The Nero pencils work well for this because they produce such nice dark tones.

Dale Jarrett and the #88 UPS Ford

11" x 14" (28cm x 36cm)
Verithin and Nero pencils on no. 3297 Arctic White mat board

COLOR USED

Verithin. Dark Umber, Carmine Red, Canary Yellow, Yellow Ochre, Indigo Blue, Orange.

Other. Nero pencils nos. 1, 3 and 4.

Using Color

Just Enough Color to Catch the Eye

This is another example of using brown tones for promotional value.

Originally created in graphite, the illustration has been gently "tinted" with a light application of brown soft pastel. It offers just enough color to catch the eye.

Dale Jarrett and the #88 UPS 2001 Ford Taurus
16" × 20" (41cm × 51cm)
Graphite and pastel on 4-ply Bristol

More Mixed Media

This drawing is another example of mixed media. This is a promotional drawing I created for a racing event in Kansas City. It combines the Kansas City skyline with interesting lettering and the speeding car. The streaking off of the car "catches" the eye and separates it from the rest of the drawing.

I created most of the drawing in just graphite, using my blending technique to give it the smooth tones. When it was finished and the graphite was sprayed, I tinted the drawing with a bit of color and colorized the lettering.

COLORS USED

Prismacolor. Crimson Red.

Verithin. True Blue, Carmine Red.

Other. Graphite.

Midwest Thunderfest Promotional Drawing
16" × 20" (41cm × 51cm)
Graphite, Verithin and Prismacolor Pencils on Bristol

Chapter Seven

TRIBUTES

Remembering Dale Earnhardt, Sr.
12" × 16" (30cm × 41cm)
Graphite on 4-ply smooth bristol
From the personal collection of Teresa Earnhardt

As an illustrator, I have one of the greatest abilities in the world. From my hand, a personal statement of someone can take shape on paper. Through my work, I am able to create an image that represents a person, that person's life and personality.

Dale Earnhardt died in an accident at the Daytona 500 in February 2001. I'll remember that day for the rest of my life. When something deeply affects me, as that day did, I immediately want to dive into my work for comfort. This drawing was my "safe place" to deal with my emotions.

The day after the Daytona 500, the feeling of loss in the NASCAR world was palpable. Even though it was still winter in the Midwest where I live, we had an unusually warm day. This was a good thing, because we had our power turned off by the city so they could work on some meters. Without power, I sat on my front porch and sketched out this portrait of Dale Earnhardt. In this piece, I wanted to represent the man we lost, not necessarily the race car driver. Instead of drawing him in uniform, with one of his penetrating gazes, I chose this pose. To me, it represents the husband, father, family member and friend.

The following pages include some of the many illustrations I have done of the drivers in the NASCAR Winston Cup Series. Most of the drawings are Officially Licensed by NASCAR, used under permission and approved by the individual teams and drivers.

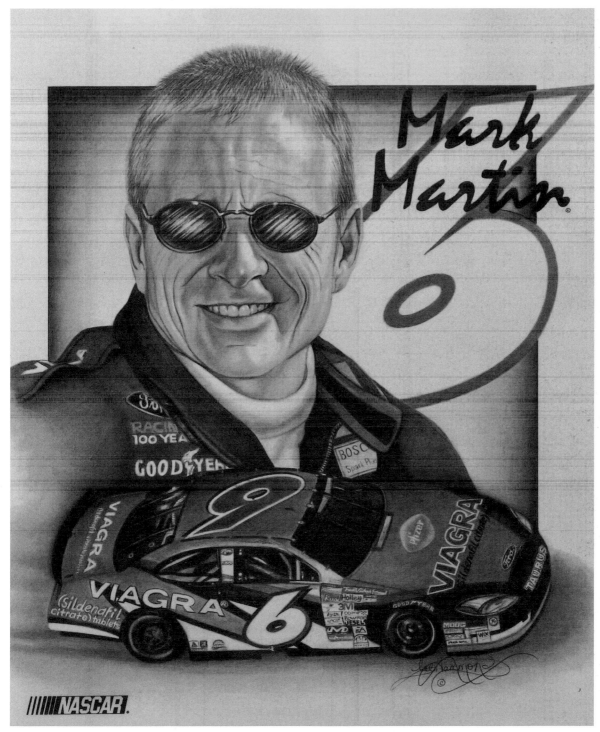

Mark Martin

Mark Martin started racing in the NASCAR Winston Cup Series in 1981. From 1989 to 2001, he maintained a consistent top-ten standing.

Driving for the Jack Roush team in 2002, Martin had a very strong year, logging twenty-two top-ten finishes. He lost the NASCAR Winston Cup title to Tony Stewart by just thirty-eight points. Still contending for the coveted Championship title, it was the fourth time that Martin has taken second-place honors.

Mark Martin

14" × 17" (36cm × 43cm)
Graphite on 4-ply smooth bristol

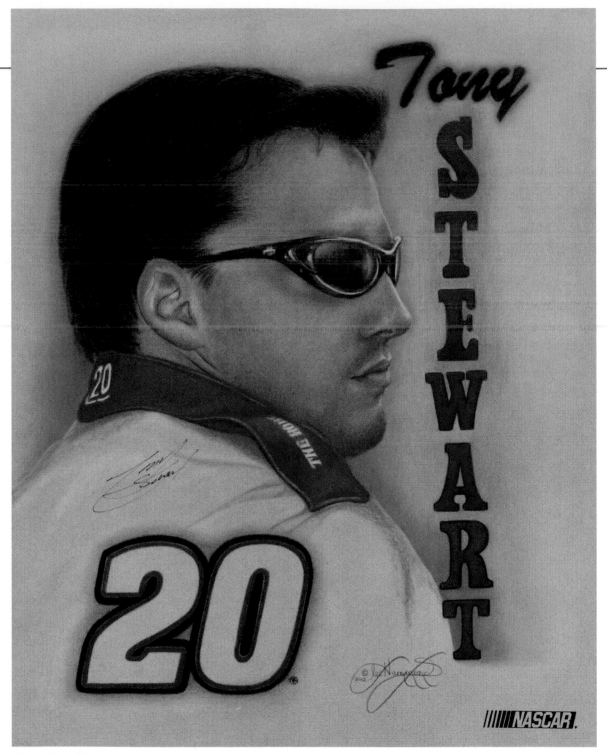

Tony Stewart

Tony Stewart is a very versatile race car driver. Although he is now known as the 2002 NASCAR Winston Cup champion, he started his racing career in open-wheeled racing with the Indy Racing League, where he won the Rookie of the Year title in 1996. In 1997 he was named Indianapolis 500 Rookie of the Year, and won the Indy Racing League championship.

He is remembered for driving both the Indy 500 and the NASCAR Winston Cup Coca-Cola 600 in the same day in both 1999 and again in 2001. In 1999, he finished ninth at Indy and fourth in the 600. In 2001, he finished both races in the top-ten.

Tony Stewart

16" x 20" (41cm x 51cm)
Prismacolor pencils on "Whisper" Suede mat board

Dale Jarrett

Dale Jarrett is a versatile athlete, and is considered a pro golfer. In his high school days he excelled in football, basketball and golf, and was even offered a full golf scholarship to the University of South Carolina.

He started his NASCAR Winston Cup career in 1984, while competing in the NASCAR Busch Series. His father, Ned Jarrett, was a two-time NASCAR Winston Cup title holder, and is now a retired television commentator for the sport.

Dale Jarrett began driving for Robert Yates Racing in 1994 and won the NASCAR Winston Cup championship title in 1999.

Jarrett is one of the most popular drivers in the NASCAR Winston Cup Series, for good reason. From 1996 to 2001, only Jarrett finished in the top-five in points every year!

Dale Jarrett 88

16" x 20" (41cm x 51cm)
Prismacolor and Verithin pencils on no.1008 Ivory mat board

Jeff Burton

Jeff Burton is a Roush Racing driver. Jeff's interest in racing began in South Boston, Virginia, at age five, watching his older brother Ward run karts. Eventually Burton began racing as well, and won the state kart championship twice. He then took the step into stock car racing.

In 1994, Burton won the Raybestos Rookie of the Year title in the Busch series, and continues to drive both NASCAR Busch and NASCAR Winston Cup to this day. In the 2000 season, Burton finished third in the NASCAR Winston Cup point standings.

Jeff Burton
14" × 17" (36cm × 43cm)
Graphite on 4-ply bristol

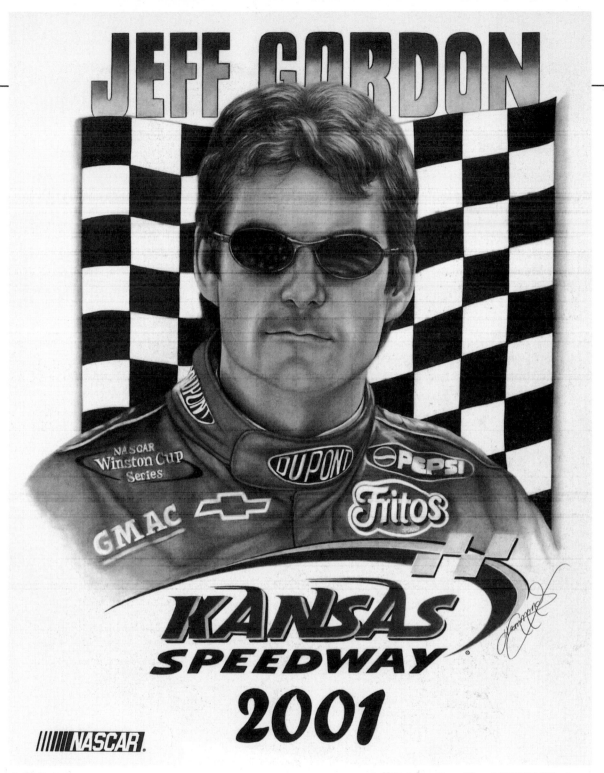

JEFF GORDON

KANSAS SPEEDWAY 2001

NASCAR.

Jeff Gordon

Jeff Gordon is one of the most popular drivers of recent history. Gordon began his racing career at age five, and excelled in open-wheel racing. During the 1970s and early 1980s, he won three national Quarter-Midget championships. He also acquired four National Karting championships. In 15 years of driving in open-wheeled competition, Gordon logged more than six hundred victories.

Gordon made his NASCAR Winston Cup debut at Atlanta in 1992, and went full time with owner Rick Hendrick in the 1993 season. He got his first NASCAR Winston Cup victory in 1994, and went on to win four NASCAR Winston Cup championships.

In 2001, Gordon won the inaugural race for the Kansas Speedway. He then went on to win the 2002 race as well!

Jeff Gordon, Four-Time NASCAR Winston Cup Champion

11" x 14" (28cm x 36cm)
Graphite on 4-ply smooth bristol

Matt Kenseth

Matt Kenseth, a Roush Racing driver, began racing at age sixteen, and is fairly new to the NASCAR Winston Cup scene. He made a grand debut in 2000, capturing the Raybestos Rookie of the Year Award.

In 2001, he finished thirteenth in the points. In 2002, he improved, maintaining an eighth-place finish in the standings, 368 points behind champion Tony Stewart.

Matt Kenseth
14" x 17" (36cm x 43cm)
Graphite on 4-ply smooth bristol

Jerry Nadeau

Jerry Nadeau started his racing career when he was only four years old, racing karts in Danbury, Connecticut. He joined the ranks of NASCAR in 1995 and competed in five NASCAR Busch Series events. Nadeau has driven for some notable team owners, including Rick Hendrick and Petty Enterprises. In 2003, he signed with MB2 Motorsports to drive the U.S. Army Pontiac, but sustained injuries when he crashed during a practice in May of that year. Nadeau has since recovered.

An Army of One
16" × 20" (41cm × 51cm)
Prismacolor and Verithin pencils on no. 1008 Ivory mat board

119

Sterling Marlin

Sterling Marlin made his NASCAR Winston Cup debut in 1976. He has two back-to-back Daytona 500 victories to his credit, in 1994 and 1995. In 2001, Marlin was hired by Chip Ganassi to drive his #40 Coors Light Dodge, which resulted in his first top-ten points finish in five years. In 2002, Sterling held the NASCAR Winston Cup points lead for twenty-five weeks, winning races at Las Vegas and Darlington. However, a late-season crash at Kansas and a neck injury took away his hopes of a first NASCAR Winston Cup title. Fully recovered, Marlin has returned for the 2003 season.

Sterling Marlin
14" x 17" (36cm x 43cm)
Graphite on 4-ply smooth bristol

Ricky Rudd

Ricky Rudd is a seasoned veteran of NASCAR. In twenty-one years, he has to his credit 763 NASCAR Winston Cup starts, 28 Bud Poles and 23 NASCAR Winston Cup victories. This earned him the Iron Man title in 2002. Rudd has driven for some of the most noted car owners in the sport, including Richard Childress, Bud Moore, Rick Hendrick and Robert Yates. He currently drives the #21 Motorcraft Ford for Wood Brothers Racing.

Ricky Rudd, Iron Man
11" x 14" (28cm x 36cm)
Prismacolor pencils on "Whisper" Suede mat board

Kyle Petty

Petty Enterprises is the most successful organization in motorsports history. Kyle Petty runs the entire organization, as well as driving a full-time NASCAR Winston Cup schedule. He made his six-hundredth career start in 2001.

His tireless hours devoted to charities have earned him the honor of being named True Value "Man of the Year" in 1998 and NASCAR Winston Cup Illustrated's "Person of the Year" in 1999.

In 1995, Petty founded "Charity Ride Across America." Over one hundred riders—including other drivers, team members and NASCAR affiliates—join in each year, riding motorcycles across the country to visit children's hospitals and participate in fund-raising. The organization has raised over $1.5 million dollars to benefit children's charities across America.

Kyle Petty
14" x 17" (36cm x 43cm)
Graphite on 4-ply smooth bristol

Terry Labonte
North Wilkesboro
April 17, 1994

Rick Hendrick
100 Victories !!!
8 Driver's, 23 tracks
1984-2001

Tim Richmond
Pocono
June 8, 1986

Hendrick MOTORSPORTS **100** VICTORIES

Darrell Waltrip
Martinsville
September 27, 1987

Ken Schrader
Talladega
July 31, 1988

Jerry Nadeau
Atlanta
November 20, 2000

Jeff Gordon
Charlotte
May 29, 1994

Ricky Rudd
Watkins Glen
August 12, 1990

Geoff Bodine
Martinsville
April 29, 1984

NASCAR is a team effort in every respect. Rick Hendrick is one of the fortunate team owners that has had the privilege of working with some of the strongest drivers in the history of the sport. In 2001, his team reached the one-hundredth victory mark. The artwork I created to commemorate this achievement depicts the drivers who combined their wins and contributed to this amazing honor. Each driver is drawn as he looked at the moment of his first win with Hendrick Motorsports. Founded in 1984, Hendrick Motorsports now fields four full-time NASCAR Winston Cup teams.

100 Victories With Hendrick Motorsports

18" x 24" (46cm x 61cm)

Graphite on 4-ply smooth bristol

From the private collection of Rick Hendrick

Conclusion

Well, here we are at the finish line! I hope you have enjoyed the ride. Much like a NASCAR driver, I am relieved to see the end, but am sad to see it come to a finish. After compiling this book and researching the facts, I am even more convinced stock car racing is the most interesting and intriguing sport in the world. It is such a rich combination of action, technical facts, science and personality.

No other sport varies as much from week to week. You never know what to expect. It is the only sport where the fans sit blended together, each rooting for their favorite team and driver, yet still considering each other friends.

As an artist, I hope I have inspired you to capture the essence of NASCAR in your own creative way. The possibilities are endless in the action-filled renderings you can create.

I hope I have presented new ideas and interesting facts about NASCAR that you may not have known. I certainly do not claim to be an expert on everything about the sport, but I sure am having fun learning as I go. I hope you will do the same.

Have fun and be creative. I'll see you at the races!

The Finish Line
The symbol for reaching the grand finale!

Victory Lane
Victory Lane and the Winner's Circle—this is what every driver wants to see at the end of the day!

The End—Crossing the Finish Line
11" × 14" (28cm × 36cm)
Prismacolor and Verithin pencils on no. 3310 Regent
Gray mat board

Glossary

Air dam. The low front spoiler of the car that directs air over or around the car (creating downforce).

Apron. The paved area directly below the racetrack that separates the track from the infield. Crossing over the yellow line onto the apron is prohibited in all cases, except in order to avoid accidents. A driver cannot use the apron to pass.

Banking. This is the degree of slope on a racetrack. It tilts inward toward the infield. Each track is different in the amount of bank. The banking helps drivers navigate the turns.

Deck Lid. This is the trunk lid of the car. It is held down with special fasteners.

Donuts. The round marks left on the side of a car from being rubbed by a competitor.

Downforce. The pressure of the air on the car as it races. Downforce actually helps the car go faster, especially with the help of spoilers, fenders and the air dam.

Drafting. Trailing a faster car and having the wind blocked is called drafting. This lessens the resistance on your car, helping you run faster.

Groove. This is the fastest path around a racetrack. It is an area of the racetrack that drivers will seek to gain track position.

Happy Hour. For one hour on Saturday night, the NASCAR Winston Cup cars are allowed to practice and final adjustments can be made to the vehicles. This is the last time the cars can be touched before the Sunday race.

Marble. During a race, chunks of rubber will come off the tires and start accumulating on the track, particularly in the corners. If a driver makes contact with these, it feels like sliding on marbles.

NASCAR. This stands for National Association for Stock Car Auto Racing.

Provisional. This is a starting place at the back of the field awarded to a driver who did not qualify for the race based on speed. To take a provisional position, a driver must be a past NASCAR Winston Cup Series champion or point leader.

Roof flaps. These are flaps on the roof of the car that flip up when a car becomes airborne. They help deflect wind to keep the car from flipping over on its top during a wreck.

Setup. During practice and qualifying, the crews "set up" the cars to work well with the track. The setup is the condition of the car right before a race. After Happy Hour, this setup is what they have to run with.

Spoiler. This is the area attached to the back of the car to deflect the wind passing over the car. It provides downforce, which help the car stay in control and improves the handling ability in the curves.

Spotter. This is a member of the team that monitors the race from a high vantage point and guides the driver through the race.

War Wagon. This is a term used to refer to the huge toolbox the crew brings to pit road. It contains everything the team needs, including tools, computers, TV, and chairs on top for the crew chief and other members.

Wedge. This describes the adjustment made to the coil springs. This alters the amount of pressure placed on the tires, by lessening or increasing the spring in the coil. The upward pressure that the spring places on the car frame is crucial to the car's handling ability.

Index

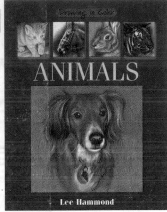

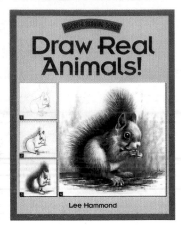

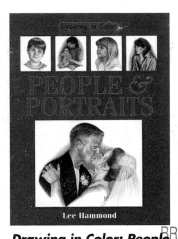

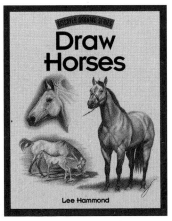